# RECONSTRUCTING YOUR WORLDVIEW

### The Four Core Beliefs
### You Need to Solve
### Complex Business Problems

## Bartley J. Madden

## Reconstructing Your Worldview

The Four Core Beliefs
You Need to Solve
Complex Business Problems

Paperback: 978-0-9885969-2-4

Hardcover: 978-0-9885969-3-1

ebook: 978-0-9885969-4-8

Published by LearningWhatWorks, Naperville, Illinois.

Printed in the United States of America.

# CONTENTS

# Chapter 4
# Systems Thinking ... 41

# Chapter 5
# Human Control Systems ... 59

# Chapter 6
# A Case Study: Free To Choose Medicine ... 71

## Chapter 7
## Worldviews and Education

*In celebration of my wife, Maricela,
and children, Gregory, Jeffrey, Miranda,
and Lucinda*

# PRAISE FOR
## *RECONSTRUCTING YOUR WORLDVIEW*

This fine book is a down-to-earth primer on what every businessperson in a dynamic economy needs to know about modern knowledge in economics, psychology, and philosophy.

—Edmund Phelps
Columbia University
Nobel Laureate in Economics

The power of this short and incisive book is its bringing together some of the key insights from neuroscience, psychology, systems thinking, and culture studies. Madden shows us how our brain, our perceptions, our prior experience, and especially our language predispose us to certain ways of thinking and acting that are not always 'realistic' or in our own best interest. With powerful organizational examples the book shows us how we can gain insight into how we function and how to improve on existing processes.

—Edgar H. Schein
Professor emeritus
Society of Sloan Fellows
MIT

The cognitive and affective suppositions that people rely upon to define 'reality' and to manage their lives is what we call a worldview. At least since Benjamin Whorf, behavioral researchers accept that worldview, language and culture are intimately linked. Much has been learned recently as is reflected in Bart Madden's excellent new book that applies the insights of brain science, linguistics and psychology to business management. Madden's book provides a cognitive roadmap to achieve triumphant strategic thinking and wealth creation.

—Werner De Bondt
Driehaus Professor of Behavioral Finance
DePaul University

What Bart Madden writes is always usefully informative and very readable, and all the more so in this book. However, even more impactful is that what he writes here provokes my own thinking. What I discover for myself out of what Bart writes makes a profound difference in my own performance beyond being merely informed, and makes a difference in my quality of life as well. I can be unreserved in recommending this book.

—Werner Erhard

I remember the first time I accessed Google Earth on my computer. Having always been interested in maps, atlases and geography, I was thrilled by the ability to look down on any part of the planet and zoom in from the broad expanse of mountain ranges, deserts and oceans to the finer details of streams, neighborhoods, city streets and individual houses. Doing so, I gained an entirely new perspective of where I lived and its relationship to the rest of the planet.

Madden's book provided me with a similar intellectual experience. Each one of us is used to seeing our world from the confines of our homes, communities and work places, a view that is largely determined today by what we have experienced in the past. We are accustomed to using certain words and phrases to describe the parts of our world, words that make assumptions about the characteristics of these parts and how they are interconnected. When something goes wrong, we often attempt to isolate the problem and come up with a quick fix without always being aware of the possible unintended consequences of our solution. And when we encounter a family member, friend or associate whose behavior is puzzling or disconcerting, we try to figure out what is making this person act the way he is.

Madden's 'Google Earth' perspective provided by his four core beliefs provides a fresh look at one's world and the assumptions one makes living in it. And this perspective includes both high-altitude perspectives of the general principles of his four core beliefs as well as zoomed-in looks at specific illustrating cases involving Wal-Mart, the smallpox vaccine, the spread of cholera, financial trading and the approval process for drugs.

We often hear today of the need to think 'outside the box' as our rapidly changing world makes current practices obsolete and poses new problems requiring innovative solutions.

Madden's book is a four-pronged tool for getting outside the box to better see what is inside and for constructing new boxes that provide better ways of meeting our objectives.

—Gary Cziko
Professor emeritus
College of Education
University of Illinois at Urbana–Champaign

Bart Madden has presented a way of thinking and real world examples that provide great insight for business leaders and business schools. The way we can become more successful as individuals, organizations and societies is to change the way we think in a positive and powerful way. The purpose of reconstructing our worldview according to Madden is about 'getting smarter' in the way we see, think and solve the complex problems in our rapidly changing business environment. This book provides a clear roadmap on how we can get smarter about the way we think about strategy and the way strategy is designed and executed. The four core beliefs presented in the book should be taught at our business schools to better enable our students to solve the complex problems confronting them now and in the future. I highly recommend this book.

—Mark L. Frigo
Ledger & Quill Alumni Foundation
Distinguished Professor of Strategy & Leadership
Director, Center for Strategy,
Execution and Valuation
Kellstadt Graduate School of Business
DePaul University

Madden provides a cognitive scaffold for a restructured worldview that will be eye-opening and valuable for all interested in improving their investments and ability to think.

—Victor Niederhoffer
Author of *The Education of a Speculator*

Bartley J. Madden's book *Reconstructing Your Worldview* is a little gem. In just a few short pages, Madden lays out four core beliefs that undergird his presentation. Madden's exposition of these four core beliefs is clear and engaging. He illustrates his points with a number of real-world examples. Madden shows the importance of worldviews by contrasting Kmart's and Walmart's business plans. A discussion of Edward Jenner's route to the development of the smallpox vaccine illustrates the role of language in both Jenner's work and that of his critics. Madden gives a number of illustrations of 'lean thinking' to show the necessity for systems thinking. Finally, he introduces the reader to perceptual control theory (PCT), a revolutionary new approach to human behavior. PCT constitutes a devastating critique of stimulus-response, linear causation dogmas in mainstream psychology. PCT provides an empirical and testable model for determining what people are actually doing and shows why most conceptions of incentives in the management literature are hopelessly inadequate. Madden brings all of these insights together in his detailed exposition of the case study 'Free To Choose Medicine.' This critique of the FDA's hidebound, costly, and sometimes deadly approach to approving new drugs is devastating.

Madden's alternative suggestions give promise of providing better drugs, sooner, at lower cost—what the Food and Drug Administration ought to be about instead of protecting its image with lengthy, costly, and often inadequate statistical tests.

Read this book. It has the potential to change your worldview.

—Hugh G. Petrie
Professor emeritus and former dean
Graduate School of Education
State University of New York at Buffalo

Bart Madden's book is well researched, well written, and highly likely to be useful to the business audience for which it is written. My own field of research is perceptual control theory, one of the four core beliefs around which Madden has structured his book. I am impressed by how clearly and accurately he explains the ideas behind perceptual control theory, and I recommend this book as an excellent introduction to the ways that incorporating this powerful theory into one's worldview can benefit the businessperson.

—Kent McClelland
Professor of Sociology
Grinnell College

# INTRODUCTION

**THIS BOOK HAS** developed over a thirty-year period beginning with my curiosity about how we know what we think we know. It's an ongoing project dealing with how we perceive the world, analyze problems, make decisions, and build knowledge. The overriding goal is to improve the handling of complex problems.

In 1991 I published an article in the *Journal of Socio-Economics* that included a section highly critical of Milton Friedman's famous methodology of positive economics. His approach dictates an extreme focus on how well a theory predicts, disregarding any skepticism concerning how reality-based its assumptions are. I sent the article to Friedman, and he replied in a letter that, pertaining to my critique of the methodology of positive economics, "I have no criticism of it, and it has no criticism of me." Apparently, Friedman agreed with my point that researchers could use this methodology to justify building fanciful and elegant mathematical models while ignoring the lack of realism of underlying assumptions; but, he implied, he himself did not do that.[1]

While my work on the topic of how we know what we think we know was progressing, my professional career was focused on investment research. My aim was an improved understanding of the causes of levels and changes in stock prices worldwide and how one could make better investment decisions for buying and selling stocks. I spent a lot of time researching systems thinking—a subject I discuss in Chapter 4—and that influenced my finance work. My 1999 book, *CFROI Valuation: A Total System Approach to Valuing the Firm,* describes a valuation framework that differs from mainstream finance in important ways, and today is used by institutional investment firms worldwide. My 2010 book, *Wealth Creation: A Systems Mindset for Building and Investing in Businesses for the Long Term,* made the case that knowledge-building and wealth creation are opposite sides of the same coin. That book contained an early version of the knowledge-building loop that I describe here in Chapter 3.

For many years I've enjoyed exploring diverse fields with the intent of formulating insights that could help with improving the handling of complex problems. This led me to the work of Bill Powers, who developed perceptual control theory (PCT), which is described in Chapter 5.

The table of contents shows what might appear to be an eclectic, unrelated group of chapters. To the contrary: I've specifically written these chapters because their very diversity supports the widespread usefulness of a reconstructed worldview. I hope to make a convincing case that the worldview-oriented material in this book leads to genuine insights for solving problems, especially complex problems in managing a business. For example, why did Sam Walton's worldview versus that of his competitors lead to Walmart's becoming the world's largest retailer? How can business schools change in order to better equip their students to solve real-world problems? What is it about a worldview that can help you solve your tough problems the same way that smallpox was eradicated and the cause of cholera discovered? This will be explained in subsequent chapters.

At the heart of this book are four core beliefs. Ideally, these core beliefs work in tandem and facilitate new, improved habits of thought. In an academic sense, I could refer to these core beliefs as propositions or hypotheses. Instead, I use the term "core beliefs" because their adoption can deliver extraordinary improvements in our thinking.

The first core belief is that past experiences shape our current assumptions. Through our assumptions about how the world works, we participate in creating what we perceive as our reality.

The second core belief is that language is perception's silent partner—silent in the sense that we are mostly unaware of the powerful influence of language. A creative use of language can generate new opportunities for a future unshackled from the past.

The third core belief is concerned with systems thinking: how to improve system performance by identifying and fixing a system's key constraints. Systems thinking helps overcome the limitations of linear cause-and-effect thinking. People often make presumed improvements to one component of a system without regard to whether this helps performance of the overall system; or they fail to identify and focus on the key constraints that are degrading system performance.

The fourth core belief is that human behavior is purposeful, and that it can be productively analyzed as a living control system. Instead of viewing behavior as a response to an external stimulus, an alternative perspective is that we compare our *actual* experiences to our *preferred* experiences and take actions in an attempt to create new experiences closer to what is preferred. The control-system perspective explains, among other things, why compensation/incentive systems often do not work well.

You may initially think that these core beliefs are a bit too philosophical, and be unconvinced as to their practical value. In this regard, I offer more detailed explanations of the four core beliefs in Chapters 2, 3, 4, and 5, and include many examples that I believe clearly illustrate their practical nature. For example, you'll gain insights about the Toyota engineer's worldview that eventually gave birth to the much-admired Toyota Production System and to the related "lean thinking" that has spread worldwide, and about Eli Goldratt's Theory of Constraints, which has been popularized in his best-selling book *The Goal*.

Chapter 6 explains the application of the core beliefs in developing a public-policy proposal of mine—Free To Choose Medicine—that could fundamentally restructure the drug-testing and approval process in the United States, much to the benefit of patients now and in the future.

Chapter 7 describes how leaders in education are shaping curriculums that address the ideas fundamental to this book, so that students are equipped with a worldview that greatly improves their innovation and problem-solving skills. This new direction isn't about conventional learning that merely looks for the right answers to textbook questions. Rather it is about creating experiences in which students learn how to ask the important, penetrating questions; how to pinpoint faulty assumptions that can be the root causes of problem situations; and how to quickly, efficiently evaluate new ideas—all critical steps for those interested in developing wealth-creating insights.

So as to present the ideas in this book in straightforward language and to avoid excessive technical details, the extensive notes serve as source material for those who want to dig deeper.

A significant portion of this book builds upon my 2012 article "Management's Worldview: Four Critical Points about Reality, Language, and Knowledge Building To Improve Organization Performance," which was published in the *Journal of Organizational Computing and Electronic Commerce.* I am grateful to Professor Mark Frigo of DePaul University for inviting me to make a series of presentations to his MBA students, who provided valuable feedback on these ideas. Two presentations were filmed and are available on YouTube, titled "Capitalism and Management's Core Responsibilities" and "Reconstructing Your Worldview." The former explains how management can run their businesses in ways that both create wealth and earn the moral high ground. The latter is an overview and application of the four core beliefs central to this book.

---

## CHAPTER 1

# SHAPING THE WORLD YOU SEE

The key to building a foundation to understand the process of economic change is beliefs—both those held by individuals and shared beliefs that form belief systems. The explanation is straightforward; the world we have constructed and are trying to understand is a construction of the human mind. It has no independent existence outside the human mind; thus our understanding is unlike that in the physical sciences.... The whole structure that makes up the foundation of human interaction is a construct of the human mind and has evolved over time in an incremental process; the culture of a society is the cumulative aggregate of the surviving beliefs and institutions.

—Douglas C. North
*Understanding the Process of Economic Change*

## A closer look at worldviews

Your worldview shapes how the world occurs to you. It influences in subtle and usually unrecognized ways the quality of your problem-solving ideas. The theme of this book is that adopting four foundational core beliefs can improve both your worldview and your handling of problems large and small. The core beliefs are foundational in the sense that they help you to pinpoint faulty assumptions that can be the root causes of a wide range of difficulties and quandaries.

Sam Walton created Walmart, the world's largest retailer. Tai-ichi Ohno laid the foundation for Toyota to become the leader in automobile manufacturing. In both cases—as discussed in later chapters—these businessmen had sharply different worldviews than those of their competitors, worldviews that resulted in significant employment gains, value to customers, and rewards to long-term shareholders. Both of these firms have had their share of public controversies in recent years. Nevertheless, it is highly informative to understand how their business models led to significant competitive advantage.

It's been my experience that the more one becomes aware of the pervasive effects of worldview on human behavior, the more one recognizes its influence literally everywhere. The many diverse examples in this book reveal what I believe are useful insights that come from analyzing worldviews. A key example is how focusing on language as a component of one's worldview can have a huge impact in developing solutions to problems. This is illustrated in Chapter 3, which describes the subtle yet powerful role of language in airplane crash investigations and how Edward Jenner was able to develop an effective smallpox vaccine.

So what exactly *is* a worldview? Basically, it's a part of, and a result of, one's process of building knowledge. It represents the ideas and beliefs with which one sees, interprets, and interacts with the world. As a familiar example, it's easy to observe how those on the far left of the political spectrum see the world quite differently from those on the far right.

The business and science examples I use illustrate how progress can be achieved with really tough problems. But it's important to keep in mind that the core beliefs are attuned to building knowledge in general and are applicable to just about any problem one encounters.

A useful way to get a handle on worldviews is to begin with the brain itself.

In order to avoid sensory overload, we operate much of the time in a kind of autopilot mode.[1] Our brains have evolved so we can act much more quickly than would be possible if every action called for conscious processing and explicit decision-making. Given that the brain has finite resources, making a process subconscious leads to increased efficiency.[2] An obvious example is that of riding a bicycle; once you've learned how to do it, your conscious mind is free to think of other things. Another of the brain's energy-thrifty strategies is to store past experiences in ways that facilitate making predictions about future events.[3] The neuropsychologist Richard Gregory notes:

> For perception, there is always guessing and going beyond available evidence. On this view, the closest we ever come to the object world is by somewhat uncertain hypotheses, selected from present evidence and enriched by knowledge from the past. Some of this knowledge is inherited—learned by the statistical processes of natural selection and stored by the genetic code. The rest is brain-learning from individual experience, especially important for humans.[4]

The neuroscientist Chris Frith puts it this way:

> By hiding from us all the unconscious inferences it makes, our brain creates the illusion that we have direct contact with objects in the physical world....

What I perceive are not the crude and ambiguous cues that impinge from the outside world onto my eyes and my ears and my fingers. I perceive something much richer—a picture that combines all these crude signals with a wealth of past experience. My perception is a prediction of what ought to be out there in the world. And this prediction is constantly tested by action.[5]

Learning about how our brains function helps us gain extraordinarily valuable insights into why we behave as we do. A very big idea, which is touched on in the introduction and explained in detail in Chapter 5, is that human behavior is purposeful: our goals—our purposes—are always in the background, guiding our actions. As such, we use variable means to achieve our goals. This contrasts with the view that behavior is merely a direct, or linear, response to an external stimulus.

Imagine that one morning your local trains aren't running because of a massive accident (stimulus) between your town and the city where you work. You decide to drive (response) to the city and although two hours late, you do make it to work. *Stimulus-response* explains your behavior—at one level of understanding.

But, depending upon your goal and the means available to you to achieve that goal, you could have behaved differently. For example, if completing a critically important memo happened to be your top priority, rather than arriving at a certain time, you might have chosen to work at home that day and email a completed memo earlier in the morning instead of spending two hours driving. Analysis of behavior focuses not so much on the actions we take, but rather on the consequences arising from our actions (staying home and finishing the memo on time).

Another term for stimulus-response thinking is *linear cause-and-effect analysis*. That is, *X* occurs, then *Y* follows. Trains are delayed and therefore you drive to work. When purpose is involved, *X* occurs and you behave, depending upon the context, in a way to best achieve your goal, which may or may not involve driving to work. But if we don't know a person's goal, we can mistakenly believe that we understand his or her behavior: the person didn't go to work and must be lazy.

## The world you see

Each of us has our own individual knowledge base. It's created from past experiences along with extraordinarily important neural connections, designed to facilitate survival, that are wired into our genetic code. As we build up our knowledge base, we automatically treat "the world out there" as an *independent reality*. And this belief is reinforced with every repeated success we have in applying linear cause-and-effect analysis to understand the world. It does not take many repetitions to learn that placing our hand on a hot stove has a painful effect.

But an even more fruitful view focuses on an awareness that an individual experiences reality as part of his or her purposeful human behavior. Such a viewpoint does not require denial of a "real world," forcing one to live a murky existence of metaphysical doubt and uncertainty. Rather, it explicitly recognizes our participation—again, consciously and/or unconsciously—in shaping the world that each of us sees as real.

The counterargument to the above point is that it is impractical, or even nonsensical, to question the reality of, say, those trees across the street. And one can unequivocally prove the reality of those trees across the street by trying to walk through them. Nonetheless, the way your brain processes the idea of "trees" is a reflection of your past experiences. At some point in your earlier life, you learned (possibly the hard way) that the trunks of trees can be firm and unyielding. We can imagine that for those who live in a jungle where safety from certain predators is obtained by climbing trees, their local language may well have assigned a word for trees that implies "safe haven." And their *reality* of trees differs from the reality experienced by those who have lived in an urban environment in which predators take different forms.

Language is intimately involved with how we experience the world. The uniqueness of something meriting a name fosters the thought that the thing has an independent existence—independent of both context and purposeful behavior—and that there is no need to think further about any assumptions behind the name. In Chapter 3 I'll discuss the subtle but important ways that language promotes the idea of an independent existence for things, thereby streamlining brain efficiency but at the same time putting up roadblocks to our knowledge-building.

That we participate in our perceptions of the world goes unnoticed because it happens, for the most part, automatically. Consider the situation where you're in a car and you decide to wait before turning left because an approaching car is too close. Unrecognized for pretty much all of us is the *learned assumption* that bigger is closer.[6] This assumption is neither recognized nor questioned for the very reason that it's proven so useful in the past. The situation is further complicated by the fact that language tends to simplify the world and, in so doing, subtly camouflages the role that assumptions play in our everyday existence. It is noteworthy that the practice of medicine is transitioning away from using terms such as "lung cancer" and "breast cancer," which merely indicate the location of one or more tumors. Instead, cancer will be labeled in ways that reveal the role of genetics and other causal mechanisms. Language refinement and knowledge-building are part of the same process.

Scientists and scholars have long addressed the notion that we actively participate in creating our reality, while examining the ways in which the use of language contributes to our knowledge base. But for those of us who are immersed in practical problem-solving, this subject matter could be dismissed as abstract, academic, or purely philosophical, and thus unworthy of our attention. The counterargument presented throughout this book is that breakthrough insights into many problem situations can occur by better understanding how we perceive the world and how we use language.

## Key points

- The impact of worldviews on our performance when dealing with problems is subtle, yet profoundly important.
- We participate in shaping the world that each of us sees as real.

## CHAPTER 2

# WORLDVIEWS

The range of what we think and do is limited by what we fail to notice. And because we fail to notice that we fail to notice, there is little we can do to change until we notice how failing to notice shapes our thoughts and deeds.

—R. D. Laing[1]

## Core Belief 1:
## Past experiences shape assumptions

How our brains function and change over time is enormously important. We know that evolution favors efficiency so that we are better equipped to survive. Our brains save energy by continually utilizing past experiences to forecast the future and by making often-used processes unconscious.

> **Core Belief 1: Our perceptions are rooted in assumptions that are based on what has proved useful in the past and are typically based on an application of linear cause-and-effect analysis (if *X*, then *Y*). However, an automatic reliance on our assumptions can inadvertently lead to bad decisions, especially so whenever a significant change in context occurs.**

As a practical matter, except for rare occasions, most of us think we are *experiencing* the world as objective reality. We are unaware of the participatory role of our assumptions. When top managers of business firms perceive their firms' competitive position based on assumptions of what has worked in their past business careers, that can often turn out to be an unreliable guidepost. It's very revealing to read the historical record of annual report shareholder letters by CEOs who have presided over a major decline and possibly the eventual bankruptcy of their firms. Typically, these CEOs assumed that the future would mirror the past, with little appreciation for their firms' changing position within the context of a complex socioeconomic system.

## Sam Walton's worldview

Walmart's success appears to be the result of providing high value to customers through low prices. But, at bedrock, I believe the primary cause of Walmart's success was a particular set of beliefs— a worldview—that was shared by managers in the firm.

In the early 1960s, Kmart was the dominant retailer in the United States and its management paid little attention to an unusually gifted entrepreneur, Sam Walton, who had started a company called Walmart—today's largest retail firm.

Before I go into more detail about how Walton grew his business, a significant point to keep in mind is that uncovering hidden assumptions is especially important for developing new ideas—ideas that greatly improve performance toward achieving a desired goal. A more efficacious worldview leads to the habit of constructive skepticism and an emphasis on in-depth analysis that can reveal the root causes of underperformance in achieving goals.

In discussing the track records of these two competing firms, it's helpful to contrast their long-term strategies during the 1970s and 1980s.

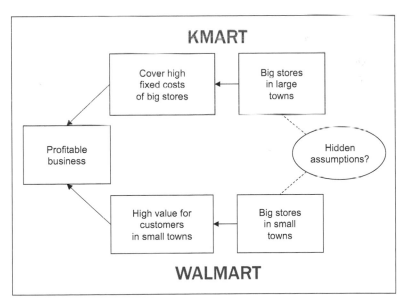

**Figure 2.1 Assumptions: Kmart vs. Walmart**

Figure 2.1 displays two different rationales for achieving a profitable retail store business.[2] In order to cover the high fixed costs of operating big stores, leadership at Kmart located their stores in heavily populated areas, where they could be sure of an immediate customer base. In contrast, Sam Walton saw an opportunity to use big stores to provide high value to customers in much less populated areas.

It should be noted that throughout his career Sam Walton was extraordinarily focused on experimenting and learning from a diversity of resources. The Walmart business model evolved not as an isolated brilliant insight, but rather as the result of much trial and error.[3] Trial-and-error experimentation resonates with how the knowledge-building process works. (I'll discuss this more fully in the next chapter.)

What were the hidden assumptions that reveal the enormous potential for wealth creation in Walmart's strategy and which explain the strikingly different beliefs—that is, worldviews—through which the managements of Kmart and Walmart interpreted and interacted with the world?

The hidden assumptions revolve around the definition of "a store."[4] In Sam Walton's worldview, each store was an integrated part of a networked system. For Kmart management, each store was viewed as a stand-alone operation in which the store manager controlled product selection, ordering, pricing, and the like. That had been a successful management philosophy, and thus Kmart's past way of doing business exerted a heavy hand in creating their collective "reality." With hindsight, we can observe how Kmart management didn't "get" Sam Walton's assumptions about how to develop and leverage competitive advantage in the retail industry. From my reading of the CEO letters to Kmart shareholders throughout the 1970s, I concluded that it was as if Walmart's business assumptions were hidden—never explicitly recognized or seriously debated by Kmart management.

In contrast, Walmart's networked system of stores and distribution centers resulted in fast-paced learning and high efficiencies tied to standardization and centralization, thereby profitably serving areas outside of major cities.[5] Over time, Walmart greatly expanded and improved its business processes at a far more rapid pace than did Kmart. In the last decade before bankruptcy, Kmart had a revolving door of new CEOs with "turnaround" plans that always focused on short-term, accounting cost reductions. That is, do what it takes to meet the accounting targets instead of placing an emphasis on process improvements that could produce solid and sustainable performance.

There was yet another aspect of Kmart management's worldview that constrained the possibilities for improving competitiveness. For Kmart management, new technology was viewed only as a means to reduce costs, whereas Walmart management perceived new technology as a potential way to improve the overall Walmart system of networked stores.[6] Consequently, when barcode scanners were introduced in the early 1980s, Walmart benefited more than Kmart. Kmart did reduce its in-store checkout costs using scanners, as did Walmart, but Kmart failed to achieve the firm-wide leverage that Walmart did. In addition to reducing checkout costs, Walmart management used the new barcoding information to feed sales data into their inbound logistics system, leading to a greatly more efficient process for maintaining just-in-time deliveries and low inventory.

Worldviews matter.

## Questioning assumptions

Strongly held but faulty assumptions that influence how we see the world are not easily dislodged. To change how people behave, I believe it is helpful to appreciate how they see the world. Compelling evidence that speaks in a forceful way to the individual is required. Often, individuals need to understand why different circumstances—that is, a changed context—have made the validity of one or more of their assumptions obsolete.

Here's an example. Every year nearly two million people become infected with HIV/AIDS in Sub-Saharan Africa. Teenage girls engaging in unprotected sex get HIV at a rate three times higher than that of teenage boys. Researchers designed a field experiment to evaluate two proposed ways to promote safer sexual behavior among young people in Kenya. An educational campaign that urged abstinence until marriage had no beneficial effect. In contrast, explaining to teenage girls that there was a much higher chance of contracting HIV from older men changed how the world occurred to these young women. The researchers used the incidence of pregnancy as a proxy for the incidence of unprotected sex that can lead to HIV. The result was a 61 percent decrease in the incidence of pregnancies in young girls associating with older, higher-risk partners.[7]

Those designing government programs would do well to avoid automatically accepting assumptions that they find plausible and appealing, and instead organize ways to build up their knowledge base through feedback from small-scale tests of key assumptions before implementing large-scale interventions.

The remainder of this chapter focuses on the scientific mindset and three main approaches used by economists to build knowledge. Each approach deals with the evaluation of assumptions that have the potential to change how we perceive the world.

The first approach is to *analyze the historical record* in order to make sense of the major economic experiences of societies over long periods of time. The second approach involves *computerized lab experiments* in order to isolate the impact of key variables that are not easily, if at all, measurable in the everyday world. The third approach focuses on designing innovative ways to run *field experiments* that can provide compelling evidence to support or reject the validity of an assumption.

Powerful new ideas can overturn existing assumptions and demonstrate that a new way of thinking leads to improved performance and better outcomes. So does this mean that all powerful new ideas warrant equal attention? No. There's a difference between an open mind and an open sink. We benefit from hard-nosed skepticism that demands confirming evidence that a new idea or hypothesis actually provides a deeper understanding and improved predictability and performance. In other words, we benefit from a scientific mindset for knowledge-building.

Before we begin examining those three approaches toward the evaluation of assumptions, let's take a closer look at the scientific mindset and its ramifications.

## Scientific mindset

In London in the mid-1800s, the death toll from cholera was horrific. The city's residents certainly benefited from physician John Snow's skepticism about the "miasma" theory, which was then widely accepted in explaining the cause of cholera epidemics.[8]

This popular theory posited that poisonous vapors—the so-called miasma—contained in foul-smelling air were the agents that caused cholera. Supporters of this theory pointed out that the poor were especially vulnerable to contracting cholera: their neighborhoods clearly had exceptionally foul-smelling air.

As cholera spread throughout London, Snow began to doubt the miasma theory. He observed that sewer workers, the group of people most exposed to the presumably noxious miasmas, did not contact cholera at a rate any higher than others who were similarly exposed. And why did some people who breathed foul-smelling air fall victim to the disease while their neighbors did not? In some prisons, the inmates rarely contracted cholera even though their environment contained the worst air in London as well as especially wretched living conditions.

To answer this question, Snow practiced the scientific principle of isolating cause and effect through a change in one variable while holding all else constant. He studied the physical networks that supplied water to London and noted that some water lines were contaminated with sewage. His hypothesis, then, was that the contaminated water was the primary cause of people contracting the disease, not poisonous air.

Snow was able to confirm this hypothesis not in the laboratory but by using field data: his was the rare situation of having the right conditions for a naturally occurring experiment. He documented that the number of cholera deaths skyrocketed the closer people lived to water pumps that were supplied with contaminated water, whereas those who drank water from pumps that were not supplied with contaminated water hardly ever contracted cholera. Because both types of pumps tended to be randomly dispersed throughout different neighborhoods, this enabled neighborhood effects to drop out (i.e., they were controlled for). Consequently, the sole focus was on whether the drinking water was contaminated or not.

## Historical analysis approach

When researchers analyze historical economic performance, all too often their political ideology guides their selection of data and their interpretations, which, to no surprise, support their deeply held assumptions about how the world works. In his book *Mass Flourishing: How Grassroots Innovation Created Jobs, Challenge, and Change*, the Nobel Prize–winning economist Edmund Phelps expresses a concern for alternative explanations of the historical record. He argues that innovation and economic growth are the result of dynamism: that is, a culture of experimentation, exploration, and imagination.

> Flourishing is the heart of prospering—engagement, meeting challenges, self-expression, and personal growth. Receiving income may lead to flourishing but is not itself a form of flourishing. A person's flourishing comes from the experience of the new: new situations, new problems, new insights, and new ideas to develop and share. Similarly, prosperity on a national scale—mass flourishing—comes from broad involvement of people in the processes of innovation: the conception, development, and spread of new

methods and products—indigenous innovation down to the grassroots. This dynamism may be narrowed or weakened by institutions arising from imperfect understanding or competing objectives. But institutions alone cannot create it. Broad dynamism must be fueled by the right values and not too diluted by other values.[9]

Phelps describes how America's rate of innovation and level of job satisfaction have declined since the 1970s. Europe has led the way to a corporatism that reveres stability and job security over creativity and change, resulting in a regrettable decline in the rate of innovation by those European firms that are stuck in business-as-usual cultures. In Phelps's view, the attitudes and beliefs of a society's members—their worldviews—are of the utmost importance, but are essentially ignored by politicians who pass legislation to "fix" the economy based on an incomplete understanding of the fundamental causes of long-term economic progress. In Phelps's words:

> My account of dynamism does not deny that science has been advancing but does not link prosperity to science. In my account, attitudes and beliefs were the wellspring of the dynamism of the modern economies. It is mainly a culture protecting and inspiring individuality, imagination, understanding, and self-expression that drives a nation's indigenous innovation.... I argue that the flourishing that is the quintessential product of the modern economy resonates with the ancient concept of the good life, a concept on which many variations have been written. The good life requires the intellectual growth that comes from actively engaging the world and the moral growth that comes from creating and exploring in the face of uncertainty.[10]

Is Phelps correct in downplaying the role of science as a contributor to economic progress? In a review of Phelps's book, the highly regarded economic historian Joel Mokyr argues that, based on his research, Phelps is wrong in downplaying the complementarities between science and business.[11] Now we confront the hard part in interpreting the historical record. Since researchers are unable to resolve differences with experiments, they necessarily need more empirical work that is not predisposed to support either Phelps or Mokyr.

In his book, Phelps employs a systems perspective; that is, an innovation is never viewed in isolation, but rather as part of a larger system. (More on systems perspectives, and their significance, in Chapter 4.) With our global economy, an innovation could be developed in one country and adopted in another. Keep in mind that innovation requires people with the capabilities not only to originate ideas but also to decide which ideas deserve funding and how to shape a business model to best advance their commercialization. This includes effective marketing to consumers who participate in the system through their willingness—or lack of willingness—to try new products and services. Also, managements need to instill a culture that motivates creative problem-solving and insightful new strategic directions.

Such a system is the heart of a modern economy's dynamism, and to achieve high dynamism, all of the system components must function well together.

Phelps's *Mass Flourishing* builds the case for hard-nosed skepticism about the top-down policies of today's politicians of every stripe. In its place, we would be best served by policies that explicitly improve dynamism in our institutions and culture. Fiscal irresponsibility, cronyism with its endless special-interest laws and regulations, and corporate short-termism have been leading the way in the opposite direction. Phelps believes that progress depends upon a deep understanding that "the genius of high dynamism [is] a restless spirit of conceiving, experimenting, and exploring throughout the economy from the bottom up—leading, with insight and luck, to innovation."

## Laboratory experiment approach

The second approach used by economists to build knowledge was pioneered by Vernon Smith. He was awarded the Nobel Prize in 2002 "for having established laboratory experiments as a tool in empirical economic analysis, especially in the study of alternative market mechanisms." Smith and many other researchers have together created a new branch of economics—experimental economics.[12] It deals with the mechanisms as to how prices are set, how people cooperate or not, and, in general, how people make decisions to create wealth for themselves. Decision-making that creates wealth is dependent upon individuals specializing in areas in which they are most skilled and participating in a society that enables voluntary exchange.

Experimental economics is uniquely suited for a variety of purposes. First, it enables one to actually experience how he or she can participate in a market-based economy and produce the economic efficiency that is described only in an abstract way in textbooks. Second, it's useful as a way to test economic theories and generate new ideas based on repetitive observed behavior. And third, it allows us to evaluate existing institutions and provide a test bed for investigating the efficiency of proposed new institutional designs.

How do laboratory experiments work? Consider a simple experiment to investigate how closely and how quickly participants—given roles as either producers or consumers in a laboratory market—achieve an equilibrium price, where supply meets demand. Each participant has his or her own computer terminal. Those who are designated as producers receive private information on their display screens about their cost to produce each unit of a traded product. Each producer is given different costs and isn't aware of either the costs of the other producers or the demands of the consumers. Producers earn the surplus of their selling price over their cost for each unit of product sold.

As for the consumers, each is informed about the values attached to each unit while not knowing what unit values are assigned to other consumers. Consumers earn real money by submitting bids to buy products, thereby enabling themselves to pocket the difference between the assigned valuation for a unit and the price paid for that unit. At the end of the experiment, cash is paid out to both producers and consumers based on what they earned.

Invariably, such an experiment produces the textbook equilibrium price very quickly, even for a small number of participants who have only limited knowledge restricted to their personal situation. Participants typically are amazed that economic theory explains their actual behavior so well—how their profit-seeking behavior collectively optimizes resource allocation and overall consumer wealth.

By running laboratory proxies for complex real-world markets, researchers can control the environmental variables and evaluate the impact of different economic environments and different institutional arrangements on market performance. The opportunities for fast-paced learning and knowledge-building are immense, including but not limited to exchange mechanisms (rules that instruct participants how to behave) for markets in financial instruments, electric power and water supply, and transportation networks. Through creative lab experiments, there is a significant learning opportunity for almost any process that involves exchange.

On one hand, care must be taken to verify that results in a lab environment can be replicated in a real-world environment. On the other hand, lab experiments can be designed to study variables that, as a practical matter, are not accessible for detailed analysis in a real-world environment.

Think for a moment about the huge spikes in electricity prices and the blackouts in California during the year 2000. The design flaws in California's system for providing electric power to consumers were magnified by a very hot summer and a particularly cold winter, a drought that crippled hydroelectric power production, power plant outages, and high natural gas prices. The resulting mess contributed to the eventual recall of Governor Gray Davis, who was replaced by actor-turned-politician Arnold Schwarzenegger, famous for his starring role in the *Terminator* movies. As to the serious system design problems, the actual need was not for the skills of a powerful robotic terminator, but for insightful, experimental economics research that was, in fact, later provided but not yet implemented.

In response to the need for policy alternatives, Professors Stephen Rassenti, Vernon Smith, and Bart Wilson at Chapman University developed a series of lab experiments in which the participants executed profit-seeking trades within various environments that represented new designs for an overall power-supply system that included the interactions of wholesale spot markets, distributors, and retail consumers.[13] One innovative idea tested was to allow for demand-side adjustment. In other words, prices to consumers would rise during peak load periods during the day, motivating them to change their habits and use less electricity when it's the most expensive.

It was demonstrated in the lab that this idea and other system changes delivered substantial gains in overall efficiency, eliminating price spikes and blackouts. Further, there was an overall reduction in costs as well as a significant reduction in the maximum capacity needed for power-generation plants.

By using experimental economics, proposed innovations can be tested and refined in an extraordinarily low-cost way. They can be offered to participants as different ways for them to make choices. For example, displaying to consumers the increased price for electricity during peak-load time periods makes them aware of a choice to reduce consumption of electricity at that time.

One would hope that an experimental mindset would be increasingly adopted by those tasked with managing large-scale power systems. In order to counteract the inertia reflected in the business-as-usual mindset, which has little regard for the costs imposed throughout the systems for which they're responsible, important observational data can be generated.

As for the need for observational data to evaluate strongly held beliefs, such as the miasma theory implicated in the spread of cholera, Smith notes the following:

> The training of economists conditions us to think of economics as an *a priori* science, not as an observational science in which the interplay between theory and observation is paramount. Consequently, we come to believe that economic problems can be understood fully by just thinking about them.... But experimentation changes the way you think about economics.... Economics begins to represent concepts and propositions capable of being or failing to be demonstrated. Observation starts to loom large as the centerpiece of economics.[14]

In terms of academic research output, experimental economics has become a growth industry, with many researchers developing insights that are not obtainable from conventional econometric analyses. A well-documented finding is that society's institutions matter because the rules they make matter. And the rules are important because incentives are important.

## Field experiment approach

The third approach used by economists to build knowledge is field experimentation. Experiments in the hard sciences typically change one variable while holding all else equal, thereby explicitly measuring the impact of the variable under study. But this is not so easy to do in complex social situations. Natural experiments like John Snow's observations about cholera are hugely informative, but they are also, as I mentioned, exceedingly rare. Hence, field experiments. While lab experiments have proved especially valuable, researchers have increasingly been running field experiments that can provide a bridge between laboratory and naturally occurring data. The power of properly designed and executed field experiments resides in their ability to foster robust confidence that one's conclusions are both sound and operationally useful since the data was obtained in a real-world environment.

A prime example is that of Louis Pasteur, whose discoveries led to the germ theory of disease and other major medical advances. He conducted a famous field experiment that illustrated the power of this technique.[15] He was challenged to prove that his recently developed vaccine for preventing anthrax from killing sheep actually worked. The experiment involved fifty sheep. Before being exposed to the deadly anthrax, half received the vaccine and the other half did not. Two days later all twenty-five vaccinated sheep were doing fine while all twenty-five controls were dead. This was compelling evidence to be sure, and in fact his experiment generated enormous interest and was reported in many newspapers. However, Pasteur's scientific mindset and his extraordinary experimental skills were not appreciated by many of his peers. Throughout his career, he was attacked by the traditional medical establishment, whose members doubted the validity of research done by a person without a medical degree. On one occasion, he noted, "I give them experiments, and they respond with speeches!"

However, unlike Pasteur's sheep experiment, studies of human phenomena invariably involve a multitude of both known and unknown variables interacting in complex ways. Consequently, field experiments need to randomize membership in both the test group and the control group in order to balance the effects of myriad variables, thereby enabling researchers to measure the effect of the single variable of interest. Ideally, participants are unaware that they are part of an experiment. Field experiments avoid many of the obstacles encountered in generalizing results obtained from lab experiments.

In their book *The Why Axis*, Professor Uri Gneezy at the University of California at San Diego and Professor John List at the University of Chicago stress that field experiments are invaluable in discovering what really motivates people and why. They remark that "business people think that running experiments is a costly undertaking, but we believe it's prohibitively costly *not* to experiment." The authors go on to describe many large-scale field experiments that are in process and that will likely provide unique insights into important societal problems. For example, depending upon past experiences, people might have huge differences in their assumptions about the extent of racial discrimination.

Professor Marianne Bertrand at the University of Chicago and Professor Sendhil Mullainathan at Harvard University ran a field experiment to shed light on this topic.[16] They sent out identical resumes to employers in response to help-wanted ads in Boston and Chicago. To isolate the variable of race perception, the researchers report that each resume was randomly assigned either a very African-American–sounding name or a very white-sounding name (as judged by the researchers). "White" names resulted in 50 percent more callbacks than did the "African-American" names. Furthermore, when higher-quality resumes were sent, the "white" resumes resulted in an additional increase of 30 percent more callbacks. But for "African-American" resumes, higher-quality ones generated little additional interest by way of callbacks. Experimental feedback can thus prove valuable by shedding light on emotional issues about which we may have strong but inaccurate or biased beliefs.

Here's another example, a rather simple study—also on the subject of discrimination—that illustrates how researchers can discover the "why" behind behavior. The first part of the experiment in this study showed that disabled people received repair quotes from mechanics for their cars that were 30 percent higher than the non-disabled.[17] Why?

In the second part of the experiment, both the disabled and able-bodied participants told the mechanics, "I'm getting three price quotes today." In this scenario there were no price differences among the quotes that were offered. The study thus revealed that the mechanics in the first experiment were simply assuming that the disabled were very unlikely to get multiple quotes and this was the cause of the perceived "discrimination." So, if a driver arrived with a car that was in such disrepair that it was unlikely to be driven any farther, we would expect this same behavior due to the same context: the lack of a competing quote.

Gneezy and List suggest that progress on big societal problems is stymied because

> ...we have failed to seek out and discover what works and why. We keep missing the opportunity to bring the tools of scientific research to understand our most pressing problems. Without understanding that life really is a laboratory, and that we must all learn from our discoveries, we cannot hope to make headway in crucial areas.[18]

## Key points

- Without our conscious awareness, our brains utilize past experiences when shaping our perceptions of the external environment—the world "out there"—as well as when making assumptions about how events and experiences will occur in the future.
- The process of knowledge-building often requires identifying strongly held, and perhaps subconscious, assumptions—some of which may be faulty.

- Studies pertaining to past events are likely to reflect the preconceived beliefs of the researcher. To counteract this tendency, the researcher needs to practice the scientific mindset of subjecting data to alternative explanations.
- Laboratory experiments and field experiments are valuable tools to help us better understand cause and effect, which in turn can strengthen our decision-making abilities.

## CHAPTER 3

# REALITY IS LANGUAGE-BASED

We live in language in the same way that fish live in water: it is transparent to us. It's not that we don't know that we speak and listen, but rather we are unaware that language is *shaping* the world as we see it. When we see the sky after an astronomer shares with us distinctions about celestial bodies, we are able to see what we were unable to see before that conversation. We see galaxies, planets, and satellites where before there were only a bunch of "stars."

—Julio Olalla[1]
*Language and the Pursuit of Happiness*

## Core belief 2:
## Language is perception's silent partner

English, like most Western languages, is rooted in linear cause-and-effect, noun-verb-noun sentence construction. And, as noted in Chapter 1, language implicitly assigns an independent existence to "things," "facts," and such. The words we choose to use can subtly promote a separation of subject versus object, organism versus environment, observer versus observed, and so on.[2] As a result, we tend to view the world through a lens of simplified and objectified noun concepts that cover up what are actually dynamic, context-sensitive processes.[3]

> **Core Belief 2: Our perceptions, our thinking, and our use of language are intertwined to such a degree that unraveling the assumptions behind the words can be a useful step in building knowledge. This also facilitates a creative use of language to generate new opportunities for a future unshackled from obsolete assumptions.**

The role of language in overly simplifying the world is illustrated in one very practical and serious problem—airplane crashes. The challenge involved in understanding what really happened goes far beyond merely pinpointing the "cause" as a mechanical failure or a human error. Sidney Dekker, an expert in analyzing human errors, notes:

> Any language, and the worldview it mediates, imposes limitations on our understanding of failure. . . . Language, if used unreflectively, easily becomes imprisoning. Language expresses but also determines what we can see and how we see it. If our metaphors encourage us to model accident chains, then we will start our investigation by looking for events that fit in that chain.

... Our most entrenched beliefs and assumptions often lie locked up in the simplest of questions. The question about mechanical failure or human error is one of them.... The question ... embodies a particular understanding of how accidents occur, and it risks confining our causal analysis to that understanding.... It sets out the questions we ask, provides the leads we pursue and the clues we examine, and determines the conclusions we will eventually draw.[4]

After Alaska Airlines flight 261 crashed in 2000, the "cause" was determined to be a mechanical failure of the horizontal stabilizer jackscrew unit due to a lack of lubrication. But the actual challenge was to gain insight into how Alaska Airlines management and maintenance employees failed to perceive the emerging safety problem. The need was to understand, from the perspective of these personnel, how they perceived the world during the many years leading up to the fatal crash.

This was a far more useful approach than simply identifying mechanical failure, which was the end result of a subtle and complex process.[5] A deeper understanding calls for using language that avoids "could have" or "should have" and instead is attuned to the context in which people behave, including the constraints on, and opportunities for, action.[6] The failure of the jackscrew unit was primarily the end result of an incremental drift over many years of making what seemed—to those involved—reasonable adjustments to maintenance procedures in order to reduce costs. But these perceived reasonable changes eventually added up to a disastrous final result. The Alaska Airlines example shows that the language we use to understand and communicate about a situation can in fact constrain our vision and interfere with knowledge-building.

## The knowledge-building loop

A creative use of language is crucial for uncovering flawed assumptions and dealing with the root causes of problems. Figure 3.1 illustrates how knowledge-building is composed of interrelated components—all influenced by language.

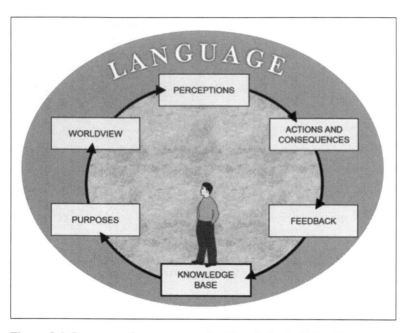

**Figure 3.1 Language Encompasses the Knowledge-building Loop**

*Source:* Bartley J. Madden, "Management's Worldview: Four Critical Points about Reality, Language, and Knowledge Building to Improve Organization Performance," *Journal of Organizational Computing and Electronic Commerce* 22 (2012): 334–346.

The effects of language apply to any kind of learning situation, whether in the context of business or science or technology or in our personal lives. Here's an example that vividly demonstrates this concept.

## Edward Jenner's path to the smallpox vaccine

In the eighteenth century, people lived in fear of a deadly disease called smallpox. Edward Jenner, a medical doctor in England, spent twenty years developing his knowledge base about smallpox, a process that led to preventative vaccination and the eventual eradication of smallpox.

The medical establishment and Jenner shared a common purpose: how best to help people avoid smallpox, which was often fatal; even those who did survive frequently suffered terrible scarring or blindness. Jenner's worldview—his ideas and beliefs for interpreting and interacting with the world—differed markedly from those of many of his medical colleagues. Jenner had a passion for observing and studying nature. His mentor was John Hunter, a noted scientist, who instilled in him the importance of generating hypotheses and experimenting.[7]

Jenner and the medical establishment had differing perceptions upon hearing milkmaids claim they didn't get smallpox because they were protected by prior exposure to cowpox. Because they milked cows, milkmaids would occasionally get cowpox, a mild disease that produced pus-filled blisters on their hands for a few weeks. Jenner was immediately interested in further investigation, while other doctors dismissed the idea. Those doctors pointed out that although some milkmaids who were exposed to cowpox subsequently avoided smallpox, other milkmaids still got it. Moreover, the other doctors' worldview was so constrained that they simply couldn't allow for the possibility that a *cow* disease could protect against a *human* disease.

But Jenner's perception of the milkmaid situation immediately led him to focus on observing actions and consequences. Specifically, he noticed that the action of exposure to cowpox sometimes had the consequence of immunity from smallpox. Jenner was skeptical about the perception of "exposure" versus the reality of "exposure." With his honed, scientific way of thinking, he was keenly aware that the use of language and our perception of reality are intertwined. To Jenner, "exposure" was not a fact, a term that neatly resolved the question, but was instead a fruitful area for investigation. Through experimentation and learning from his mistakes, he discovered that there were many cowpox-like diseases, but only one could protect against small-pox. Furthermore, he discovered that it was the large, bluish blisters that occurred midway through the cowpox cycle that contained the pus that was potent enough to protect against smallpox.

Jenner's worldview facilitated his investigation of new relationships that did not fit within existing medical knowledge—as opposed to the worldviews of many of his medical peers. In fact, when he submitted a paper reporting his findings to England's Royal Society, this remark was part of the reply: "[He] would more likely keep his colleagues' esteem in this respectable society by withdrawing his manuscript and forgetting about it as quickly as possible."[8] However, this faulty appraisal of Jenner's work was soon forgotten in the wake of the demonstrated health benefits achieved from following his recommendations.

By the time Edward Jenner died in 1823, he was widely acknowledged and even revered as the conqueror of smallpox. Vaccine technology improved over time and in 1967 the World Health Organization began a campaign to totally eradicate smallpox. In 1977, the last person to become infected with smallpox was reported in Somalia, Africa.

As with Sam Walton many years later, Jenner's observations and experiments provided feedback to him that, over time, continually improved his knowledge base. Business leaders who instill a knowledge-building loop as part of their firm's culture—a continuous cycle of shared learning that is enthusiastically embraced by employees—tend to create substantial wealth over the long term.

## Design thinking

The Edward Jenner anecdote is but one example of the knowledge-building loop in operation in scientific work and demonstrates the importance of both language and context. The same loop process is also reflected in innovative design work. Tim Brown,

CEO of the preeminent design firm IDEO, describes how designers in his firm work:

> Design thinking is inherently a prototyping process. Once you spot a promising idea, you build it. The prototype is typically a drawing, model, or film that describes a product, system, or service. We build these models very quickly; they're rough, ready, and not at all elegant, but they work. The goal isn't to create a close approximation of the finished product or process; the goal is to elicit feedback that helps us work through the problem we're trying to solve. In a sense, we build to think.[9]

In their book *Creative Confidence: Unleashing the Creative Potential Within Us All,* Tom Kelley and David Kelley describe many insightful examples of design practice at IDEO and at the Hasso Plattner Institute of Design at Stanford University, commonly referred to as the d.school. Particularly important is the questioning of assumptions through field observations and prototyping. Here are a few examples of this innovative mindset.

One IDEO assignment was to solve a problem for surgeons whose hands became tired from using an existing dissection tool for sinus operations. The client asked for a new design to make the tool lighter. It would be easy to apply linear cause and effect and conclude that a heavy tool makes a surgeon tired. But recall the point made in Core Belief 2 that our perceptions, our use of language, and our thinking are intertwined to such a degree that unraveling the assumptions "behind the words" can be a useful step in building knowledge.

Seeing behind the words to question assumptions is integral to innovative design. So, instead of an excessive concern with the words "weight reduction," IDEO designers focused on the desired end result of improving overall functionality and making the surgical tool considerably more comfortable for surgeons during long procedures. This led to many more potential solutions to the core problem. The final redesigned tool received rave reviews from surgeons even though it weighed a few grams *more* than the original tool.

The second example involves four students in a design course at the d.school who began work on an unusually important problem. Every year, one million low-birthweight babies die from hypothermia because they don't have enough fat to control their body temperature. Half of this death toll occurs in India. Hospital incubators can provide the monitored heat necessary to save these babies, but the machines can cost as much as $20,000.

The *perception* of this design problem was crucial. It was improved by seeing up close what is actually happening in India, which one of the students was able to do. The facts on the ground were that for cultural reasons, the hospital incubators were going unused because mothers were motivated to keep babies in their homes and away from the hospitals. The design challenge then became how to develop a radically low-cost baby-warming device for use in mothers' homes.

The students' prototype for their class was later more fully developed into the Embrace infant warmer that cost 99 percent less than a conventional incubator. It is an understatement to say this product is a lifesaver.

## Ray Dalio's principles

Because knowledge-building and wealth creation are tightly connected, we should be able to observe business organizations achieving extraordinary performance over time due to excellence in knowledge-building. Along these lines, consider Ray Dalio, the founder and architect of Bridgewater, the world's largest and most successful hedge fund management firm. The firm's performance has been exceptionally rewarding for its clients. Bridgewater funds are noted for delivering substantial excess returns that are mostly uncorrelated with the general market, and the firm's stellar performance has been maintained even as its assets grew to $150 billion.

Dalio has created a unique culture for the firm's 1,400 employees. It is built upon independent thinking, radical openness, an extraordinary focus on learning from mistakes, and a striving for an effective analytical approach that provides insights about the drivers of economic performance across different countries and time periods—in short, a knowledge-building culture. He has compiled an extensive document, *Principles,* that can be downloaded from Bridgewater's website. This document describes Dalio's approach to success in living one's life, and includes content on how he manages Bridgewater.

In reading his *Principles,* I observed a strong connection to ideas similar to the ones that are the focus of this book. Here are some excerpts:

> People who worry about looking good typically hide what they don't know and hide their weaknesses, so they never learn how to properly deal with them and these weaknesses remain impediments in the future.

> The main reason Bridgewater performs well is that all people here have the power to speak openly and equally and because their views are judged on the merits of what they are saying. Through that extreme openness and a meritocracy of thought, we identify and solve problems better. Since we know we can rely on honesty, we succeed more and we ultimately become closer, and since we succeed and are close, we are more committed to this mission and to each other. It is a self-reinforcing, virtuous cycle.

> Create a culture in which it is OK to make mistakes but unacceptable not to identify, analyze, and learn from them.... [S]chool learning overemphasizes

the value of having the right answers and punishes wrong answers. Good school learners are often bad mistake-based learners because they are bothered by their mistakes. I particularly see this problem in recent graduates from the best colleges, who frequently shy away from exploring their own weaknesses.[10]

Dalio discusses how faulty thinking results from using words without examining the assumptions behind them. He focuses on the word "correlation." Here is Dalio's reasoning:

> People think that a thing called *correlation* exists. That's wrong. What is really happening is that each market is behaving logically based on its own determinants, and as the nature of those determinants changes, what we call correlation changes.[11]

What Dalio says is reminiscent of the point that the uniqueness of something meriting a name fosters the erroneous thought that the thing has an independent existence—independent of context and purposeful behavior—as well as the false idea that there's no need to think further about any assumptions behind the name.

Dalio notes that in an environment of volatile expectations for economic growth, stocks and bonds will tend to be negatively correlated. But in an environment of volatile inflation expectations, stocks and bonds will tend to be positively correlated. He stresses the need to deal with causality and not to be misled by language that can oversimplify. Correlation depends upon context.

Earlier in the book, I remarked that the core beliefs may seem a bit philosophical but are, in fact, highly suited for making progress with pressing practical challenges, such as performance improvement. The important new work of the Barbados Group is highly compatible with Core Beliefs 1 and 2 in particular, and warrants a closer look.

## Barbados Group

Werner Erhard, Michael Jensen, and their Barbados Group colleagues—hereafter simply termed "EJB"—have developed a new paradigm for individual, group, and organizational performance. The theoretical underpinnings of this approach are covered in a series of working papers available on the Barbados Group's website.[12] EJB's new paradigm emphasizes how a person's worldview shapes and constrains his or her perceptions.[13] Their paradigm dives deep to the source of performance, which is not accessible by mere linear cause-and-effect analysis—as noted earlier in this chapter in the section about the failure of the jackscrew unit on Alaska Airlines flight 261.

EJB assert that the level of performance that people achieve correlates with how work situations occur to them. Additionally, language—including what is said *and* unsaid in conversations—plays a dominant role in how situations occur to the performer. Therefore, substantial gains in performance are more likely to be achieved after management gains an insightful understanding of how employees perceive the world and then orchestrates changes that make sense to employees and elicit enthusiastic support. EJB make the following distinctions to explain the logic of their approach to improving performance:

> Action is a correlate of the way the circumstances on which and in which a performer is performing *occur* (show up) for the performer.... "Occur" does not require the performer to pay any attention to, think about, understand, analyze, or interpret that which is registered.

> ... The world we *interact* with (act on and by which we are acted on) is the so-called objective world.

However, while most of us don't give any thought to it, in a fundamentally important sense the world we actually *respond to* and *react to* is the world as we perceive it, what we have termed the *occurring* world.

... [If] we are dealing with life *as lived*, or performance *as lived* (the perspective of this new paradigm of performance), seeing and treating the objective and occurring worlds from the perspective of them being two distinct *and* separate worlds obscures the way we actually live life and live performance.... [T]he *as-lived* perspective allows access to the *source* of performance.[14]

An insightful presentation of the application of these ideas is provided by Barbados Group members Steve Zaffron and Dave Logan in their book *The Three Laws of Performance*. Zaffron and Logan describe how employees—and people in general—have a deeply felt default future: that is, what they *believe* they know will happen. This strongly influences how the world occurs to them and, hence, their performance.

We all use descriptive language to create "facts" and to describe our reality; this type of language, more often than not, binds and constrains us. Rewriting the future involves dealing with the past so that it no longer constrains us. In this way we can create space for new possibilities. Rewriting our default future involves generative language—a language composed of declaration, commitment, promises, and requests.[15] Generative language is really about transforming, rather than describing, how a situation occurs.

A future we create for ourselves and others, one that offers high potential rewards for everyone involved, is most likely to be achieved, say Zaffron and Logan, through effective leadership. This entails that: (1) leaders have a say, and give others a say, in how situations occur; (2) leaders master the conversational environment; and (3) leaders listen for the future of their organization. In a nutshell, the success of managers' change initiatives depends upon how successfully they analyze how the world occurs to their employees.

A centerpiece of EJB's new paradigm is its emphasis on integrity, on keeping one's word; this has a significant impact on performance. Jensen says it well:

> Integrity is important to individuals, groups, organizations and society because it creates *workability*. Without integrity, the workability of any object, system, person, group or organization declines; and as workability declines, the opportunity for performance declines. Therefore, integrity is a necessary condition for maximum performance. As an added benefit, honoring one's word is also an actionable pathway to being trusted by others.[16]

There is much more involved with the EJB paradigm than can be covered in this short summary, especially regarding their approach to leadership training. An issue that initially comes to mind is the application of this mindset vis-à-vis the alignment between employees' personal goals—their purposes—and management's goals for the firm. The following example illustrates the fundamental EJB focus on how the world occurs to people.

In her book *The Measurement Nightmare: How the Theory of Constraints Can Resolve Conflicting Strategies, Policies, and Measures,* Debra Smith describes a situation in which a plant's key constraint was that some complex machinery was frequently down due to mechanical problems.[17] Management had been measuring the performance of maintenance personnel by how long it took them to get the machinery back up and running after a breakdown. Then management changed the performance measurement to how long the machinery was operational between breakdowns. This *changed the way the world occurred* to maintenance personnel and motivated them to focus much more earnestly on discovering the root causes of breakdowns and how to prevent them. The result was longer run-times between breakdowns—and higher productivity.

## Key points

- Language subtly shapes the world we see and its use can easily oversimplify complex relationships to a degree that interferes with developing innovative solutions to problems.
- How we use language in developing and communicating ideas is crucial to overcoming preconceived faulty beliefs as well as testing new assumptions.
- The prototyping process used by designers has a far wider use to all of us: the process utilizes a specific kind of language to express ideas and generate fast feedback.
- A better future is more readily achieved by discarding language that cements us to a status-quo past environment and, instead, using language attuned to new possibilities.

## CHAPTER 4

# SYSTEMS THINKING

The secret to being a good scientist, I believe, lies not in our brain power. We have enough. We simply need to look at reality and think logically and precisely about what we see. The key ingredient is to have the courage to face inconsistencies between what we see and deduce and the way things are done. This challenging of basic assumptions is essential to breakthroughs. Almost everyone who has worked in a plant is at least uneasy about the use of cost accounting efficiencies to control our actions. Yet few have challenged this sacred cow directly. Progress in understanding requires that we challenge basic assumptions about how the world is and why it is that way. If we can better understand our world and the principles that govern it, I suspect all our lives will be better.

—Eliyahu M. Goldratt
*The Goal: A Process of Ongoing Improvement*

Like all systems, the complex system is an interlocking structure of feedback loops.... This loop structure surrounds all decisions public or private, conscious or unconscious. The processes of man and nature, of psychology and physics, of medicine and engineering all fall within this structure.

—Jay W. Forrester
*Urban Dynamics*

## Core Belief 3:
## Improve performance by identifying
## and fixing a system's key constraints

We go through life experiencing discrete events in which an effect has a single cause. And the cause immediately precedes the effect that surfaces. Consequently, we tend to perceive problems as isolated events, and our natural inclination is to simplify situations by using linear cause-and-effect analysis—the old reliable tool that has served us so well in the past. But life, of course, is not always simple; rather, it is full of complex events and systems.

**Core Belief 3: Systems thinking is invaluable as a means to complement linear cause-and-effect analysis applied to isolated components of a system, to address the tendency toward an excessive focus on local efficiencies that can easily degrade overall system performance, and to powerfully identify and focus on fixing the key constraints to achieving the system goal.**

A system is a group of interdependent components, typically having complex feedback loops, that form a unified whole with a common purpose, such as the human body or a business firm. Systems thinking is a way to understand and communicate about the dynamic complexities and interdependencies involved.[1] In many complex systems (such as ecological ones like rainforests), when you have nonlinear cause-and-effect relationships with varying time lags and multiple feedback loops, a simplified, linear cause-and-effect analysis is insufficient for predicting a system's behavior. The whole system behaves in ways that cannot be reduced to just an analysis of isolated system components.

Nevertheless, as we increase our understanding of any system, our perceived level of the system's complexity declines. To be sure, there are actually simple principles at work in complex systems, such as airplanes, that produce reliable cause-and-effect relationships. The design of a wing for a specific airplane type is a complicated engineering task. But Bernoulli's equation for fluid flow is a simple principle that relates velocity to pressure and explains how to design airplane wings to produce lift. However, when those who are designing changes to a complex system, like an airplane, are uninformed about foundational principles, you can expect bad results.

The applicability of systems thinking to improve performance is both extraordinarily wide and keenly important. In this chapter, I limit my focus primarily to the business world. It's my strong belief that every organization that has a defined goal can benefit from systems thinking. As the Walmart/Kmart example in Chapter 2 illustrated, tremendous wealth can either be created or dissipated by managements who either "get it" or don't in regard to systems thinking. Managements who don't "get it" regarding a long-term systems perspective invariably are excessively focused on quarterly earnings reports. Unfortunately, managements who assert that employees must do whatever it takes to "make the accounting numbers" are all too easy to find. The undesirable result is an extreme focus on meeting or exceeding Wall Street's quarterly earnings expectations, accompanied by a loss of integrity and all sorts of quick fixes that are the antithesis of a continuous process-improvement environment that is emblematic of lean, effective organizations such as Toyota.[2]

Systems thinking offers extraordinary leverage for improving organizational performance. Early on, Walmart management adopted a systems view and revolutionized the retail industry while creating enormous wealth. Another striking example comes from the airline industry. In sharp contrast to its major competitors who viewed the world in terms of maximizing the operating efficiency of their airplanes, management at Southwest Airlines (SWA) defined system efficiency from the perspective of their customers' starting points and destinations. This led to an organizational structure that enabled many direct flights to smaller cities, which were profitable as well as especially valued by customers. SWA's major competitors relied on a hub-and-spoke organization, which focused on major cities and was ill-suited to serving the same customers that SWA targeted. For many years, SWA's profits have routinely exceeded the combined total of all of its competitors' profits. Breaking the hold of a faulty system assumption that has become an integral part of an industry's culture can lead to a high-performance strategy that is difficult for competitors to copy.

## Lean thinking

Managements worldwide have recognized the superior operating performance of preeminent lean companies such as Toyota and Danaher and have embraced lean principles for running their own firms. In their book *Lean Thinking: Banish Waste and Create Wealth in Your Corporation,* James Womack and Daniel Jones explain the five key lean principles as follows: "precisely specify *value* by specific product, identify the *value stream* for each product, make value *flow* without interruptions, let the customer *pull* value from the producer, and pursue *perfection*."

They describe a value-stream project undertaken by Pratt & Whitney, a large manufacturer of jet engines and a division of United Technologies. An overall systems view that focused on waste revealed that many activities undertaken by their raw-material suppliers were duplicated by the next firms downstream as part of the process to produce ultrapure metals that were to be machined into aircraft parts. Initially, the ingots of expensive titanium and nickel were manufactured in massive sizes. This practice was found to cause 90 percent of the ingots being scrapped, in addition to many unnecessary work activities. Instead of seeing reality as a value stream that encompasses the entire production process culminating with the end customer, the forging and melting firms' managers had perceived their activities as independent of other activities along the value stream. Subsequent modifications in Pratt & Whitney's requirements, along with a redesign of the ingots with attention paid to the shape of the finished parts they were being made for, brought about dramatic reductions in both wasted material and time.[3]

Lean-oriented managers, studying every activity leading to the delivery of a final product, look for *muda,* the Japanese word for waste. *Muda* is any activity that adds no value but is currently part of the work process. Womack and Jones report that a typical walk along a non-lean firm's value stream shows that more than 80 percent of the total steps are, in fact, *muda*: waste.

Lean management involves a business culture that differs markedly from a conventional command-and-control hierarchy in which managerial "skill" is viewed as successful firefighting and workarounds to do whatever it takes to meet targeted accounting results. Instead, a lean culture focuses on continuous process improvement through work specifications that provide stability to a process. And this is followed by experimentation using a scientific approach for analyzing cause and effect in order to obtain even further process improvement. Instead of telling employees how to fix problems, lean managers engage employees in constructive dialogues about the potential root causes of problems. One result of guiding/mentoring employees in their improvement efforts is that both process improvement and employee learning are jointly achieved.

A lean culture has a horizontal orientation in order to better coordinate work and reduce waste along the entire value streams that end with the customers. The focus is on optimizing the entire system to deliver value to the customer. In contrast, a command-and-control orientation is composed of vertical silos with incentives to improve local efficiencies.

## Ohno's circle

What is the source of the lean revolution that we see improving performance worldwide in manufacturing plants, service operations, and all sorts of other complex business systems? The typical answer is that the Toyota Production System was the birthplace of lean. If you dig even deeper, you'll find that the real source was one man: Taiichi Ohno, a Toyota engineer, whose perceptions of the workplace were enormously insightful. Ohno's worldview gave enormous credibility to microscopic observation of work within the context of the overall system and to identifying non–value-adding activities. His perception of reality, like Edward Jenner's, differed radically from that of his contemporaries.

In the aftermath of World War II, the automotive industry in Japan faced low demand and needed to produce only small quantities of a wide variety of vehicles. Capital was scarce. Due to these circumstances, Ohno pioneered the fundamental lean principle of continuous flow—as opposed to the mass-production processes used in the United States. He stated his goal in simple terms:

> All we are doing is looking at the time line from the moment the customer gives us an order to the point when we collect the cash. And we are reducing that time line by removing the non–value-added wastes.[4]

Ohno developed a systematic method for continuously identifying and eliminating waste. He implemented standardized work processes and instilled a culture of employee involvement and mentoring so that employees had the skills to find the root causes of problems and to implement and verify solutions. In this environment he then continuously reduced inventory levels in order to see where waste existed. Instead of accepting the accountants' standard language of inventory as being an *asset*, he viewed inventory as a *liability* that masked problems and interfered with achieving continuous flow and concomitant waste reduction.

Many of the Toyota employees mentored by Ohno were put inside a circle that Ohno drew on the plant floor and were then instructed to observe a problem situation. One senior Toyota managing director has this to say about his experience, early in his career, in the Ohno circle:

> So I went into the circle and began to watch the process. During the first hour, I began to understand the process. After two hours, I began to see the problems. After the third and fourth hours, I was starting to ask "why?" Finally, I found the root cause and started to think about countermeasures. With the countermeasures in place, I reported back to Mr. Ohno what I had observed and the problems I saw and the countermeasures I put in place as well as the reasons for the countermeasures.
>
> Mr. Ohno would just say, "Is that so?" and nothing more. He never gave us answers. Most of the time he wouldn't even tell us if what we did was good or bad. Now I realize what Mr. Ohno was trying to do. He was trying to make us think deeply—and think for ourselves.[5]

As for thinking for ourselves and getting to the root causes of fundamental business problems, we all can benefit from going to the *gemba:* a Japanese word for "the real place." In a business operation the *gemba* is where the actual work is done.

### *Gemba* walks

The intellectual leader of the lean movement, management expert James Womack, notes that early in his career when he worked at a university, his routine was to use accepted theory as a lens to analyze the data that was available to him. That routine changed when he learned about the benefits of Ohno's advice to directly observe how work is being done and only then formulate hypotheses about how best to orchestrate improvements.

If Guinness World Records had a category for visiting companies and following a single product family along its entire value stream to see where more could be achieved for less, Womack would hold that record forevermore; he is a master at the *gemba* walk. A *gemba* walk is all about questioning not only the efficiency of the processes that make up a value stream but, at a deeper level, learning to what extent a process is really attuned to delivering genuine value in the eyes of customers.

Womack stresses the importance of mutual respect between management and employees, nurtured by their active participation in problem-solving. This yields improvements that could not otherwise be achieved. Joint participation in process improvement generates sustained innovation and creativity.

Womack describes *gemba* walks of his that involved two distribution centers in the same city, both providing essentially the same service. The two sharply different management approaches provided a useful experimental lens through which to compare a non-lean approach versus a lean approach. Womack noted that these facilities had similarly educated employees and similar employee compensation. Managers of the first facility set goals with little regard for how results were achieved. Further, they didn't involve employees in joint efforts to discover the root causes of problems in order to improve processes. Instead, managers were busy with firefighting and workarounds. A hallmark of this facility was a lack of standardization of the work processes.

In contrast, managers of the second facility instilled lean practices, with highly visible readouts of how standardized work was progressing. Every employee spent four hours a week with his or her line manager, analyzing the root causes of inefficiencies in processes, implementing changes, and evaluating results.

The non-lean facility had an annual turnover of 70 percent and roughly half the productivity of the lean facility. Significantly, the personnel of the lean facility, with a miniscule annual turnover, exhibited enormously higher job satisfaction. When Womack inquired about their job satisfaction, the reply was "The work here is always challenging because we are always solving problems using a method we all understand. And we all respect each other's contributions."[6]

It seems clear to me that this example highlights the business-oriented, bottom-up path, one by which a society can achieve the dynamism and mass flourishing that Edmund Phelps describes so eloquently as coming from "the experience of the new: new situations, new problems, new insights, and new ideas to develop and share."

## The Theory of Constraints

In the realm of solving business problems, Eli Goldratt has offered unique contributions. Many have been introduced to his Theory of Constraints (TOC) framework through his enormously popular book *The Goal: A Process of Ongoing Improvement.*

All too frequently, an accounting-based performance scorecard for one part of a manufacturing process motivates those responsible for the work to reduce accounting costs without regard to effects elsewhere or consideration of alternative uses of resources. This is because they think narrowly and focus on the measured local efficiency—the work activity—that would improve if costs decline. But Goldratt and other systems thinkers disagreed. They emphasize that optimizing local efficiencies is not at all the same as optimizing the overall system.

The problem here is that of a hidden assumption lurking in the background. Note that for accountants and users of accounting-based reports, the word "cost" implies that less cost is good and more cost is bad—a prime example of how language simplifies. But their conclusion can only be right if system components are really independent of one another such that the sum of local efficiencies directly translates into efficiency of the entire system. It's a faulty assumption because system components are actually interdependent. A classic example is a manufacturing line where the key constraint is, say, machine B. Although the installation of a more efficient and faster machine at A upstream—which feeds into B—will improve A's performance, this can easily make matters worse for B and degrade the overall system's performance.

If one has a worldview that puts accounting costs foremost, then there are endless opportunities to reduce these costs. In contrast, Goldratt was relentless in promoting the need for an extreme focus on identifying and fixing the key constraint at a point in time and then moving on to identifying where the constraint has now moved in order to repeat the performance-improvement process. For example, as large-scale improvements are made in manufacturing plants, the key constraint might move outside the plant to the firm's marketing process, where scrutiny could next focus.

In my opinion, Goldratt's most important contribution is the TOC thinking processes. In the most fundamental terms, the primary TOC objective is to answer three questions:

(1) What to change?
(2) Change to what?
(3) How to cause the change?

This is a departure from standard approaches to problem-solving, especially those seen in economics and finance that set up a problem as one of maximizing some variable given existing constraints. Goldratt was adamant that such compromises, based on accepting constraints, should be avoided. Instead, one should devise logical maps to help generate insights, enabling one to dissolve conflicts and any related compromises. TOC logical maps begin with undesirable effects (UDEs) and trace important cause-and-effect relationships, all the while scrutinizing assumptions that are seldom questioned or even recognized. As one's skill in using TOC tools improves, one is better able to discover one or more faulty assumptions that lead to UDEs and conflict situations. Breaking the hold of faulty assumptions is how compromises can be avoided and system performance significantly improved.

Of course, business systems are complex, but the beauty of TOC thinking tools is in how complexity is handled by dealing with primary cause-and-effect relationships in a systematic and visual way. For the user of TOC logical maps, reality changes. One is able to see the process by which UDEs surface. The various types of TOC logical maps yield insights that are, in fact, simple and, as Goldratt frequently remarked, represent common sense. In particular, TOC's "current reality tree" and "future reality tree" represent an insightful way to communicate the steps necessary for people to achieve a future that eliminates the UDEs that degrade the current situation. People are more likely to "buy into" a proposed transition when the logic underlying the trees, or maps, is so compelling that the transition appears to simply reflect common sense.

What follows is from my own experience and shows an application of the most basic TOC thinking tool—the Evaporating Cloud, which was so named by Goldratt to reflect how a conflict situation can evaporate once a faulty assumption is revealed.

## Evaporating Cloud and stock trading

In the early 1990s, I was concerned with a fundamental conflict that confronts portfolio managers who want to make either a large purchase or a large sale of stock. In a journal article I outlined the conflict and proposed a solution along the lines of TOC thinking, focused on discovering the faulty assumption that could resolve the conflict.[7]

Consider the manager of a mutual fund who wants to sell 800,000 shares of a stock that has an average daily trading volume of 100,000 shares. Hoping to avoid putting excessive downward pressure on the stock, that manager could sell, say, 20,000 shares per day, which would take forty days to liquidate the position. But in this scenario, the manager receives sale proceeds slowly over the forty-day trading period and therefore would be unable to quickly use the full sale proceeds to buy stock with perceived better prospects. In an alternative scenario, the manager could make a block trade of the entire 800,000 share position and receive the sale proceeds as soon as this single transaction settles.

The problem lies in communicating that there's a large block to sell. When this happens, information is leaked to market participants who can "front run"—that is, they can profit by selling in advance of the block trade, anticipating that the block trade will further depress the stock. For those who manage sizable stock portfolios, this is a deeply felt, repetitive conflict situation.

The conflict is depicted in Figure 4.1.

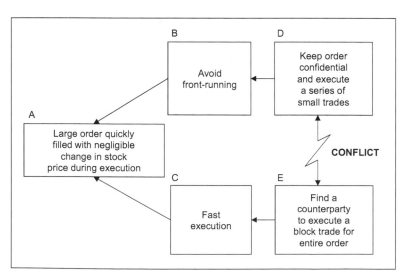

**Figure 4.1 Evaporating Cloud for Large Block Trades**

To achieve the portfolio manager's objective, which is shown in the far left box, "A," the manager needs to avoid front-running, "B," but still obtain fast execution, "C." In order to avoid front-running, the manager wants to avoid leaking news of the big order and hence is inclined to execute a series of small orders, "D." But the need for fast execution means that the manager is also inclined to reveal the entire order in hopes of finding a counterparty to then execute a fast block trade for the entire order, "E."

There are assumptions hidden in Figure 4.1 that are the presumed reasons why a necessary condition exists for each action. Articulating the hidden assumptions can reveal that at least one of them is erroneous; this can lead to dissolving the conflict and avoiding a compromise.[8]

My analysis suggested that the key erroneous assumption was that finding a counterparty for a block trade requires the portfolio manager's trading desk to reveal both the size of the order and whether it's a buy or sell. I proposed a "yellow-light trading" system that could enable institutional traders to observe that a large order for a particular stock was in the system without revealing the order size or whether it was a buy or sell, thereby avoiding front-running. The ticker symbols for the stocks with large, pending block trades would be highlighted in yellow on the traders' terminal screens. A trade is consummated if and when a counterparty inputs the opposite side at a mutually agreed-upon price. In 2004, Pipeline Trading Systems implemented my yellow-light trading concept.[9] Its business grew at a very rapid rate as institutional money management firms greatly benefited from the use of this new type of trading platform. Regrettably, the firm eventually had to be shut down because of unethical practices that violated the fundamental requirement of confidentiality.

## Problem-solving nature's way

Systems thinking is ideally suited to solving problems and, as has been mentioned, has enormously wide application. Often, knowledge advances because of a creative use of systems thinking that reveals an assumption of independence as being inadequate. Consider the widely held assumption that our brains are similar to computers: they receive signals from our senses and create internal representations of the world. Then the brain figures out what is best to do and sends back signals in order to initiate the presumably appropriate actions. Viewed from this perspective, the brain is a "stand-alone" computer.

An alternative embedded-cognition perspective is that the body, the brain housed within it, and cognition are part of a dynamic system connected to the world we inhabit. This perspective is far more meaningful and useful; it leads us to be less concerned with how representations of the world get into our head, and much more concerned with adaptive loops of behavior, which focus on the control of our perceptions of the variables that are important to us. (More about this in the next chapter.)

Andy Clark, a professor of logic and metaphysics at the University of Edinburgh, summarizes this perspective as follows:

> Perception is commonly cast as a process by which we receive information from the world. Cognition then comprises intelligent processes defined over some rendition of such information. Intentional action is glossed as the carrying of commands that constitute the output of a cogitative, central system. But real-time, real-world success is no respecter of this tripartite division of labor. Instead, perception is itself tangled up with specific possibilities of action— so tangled up, in fact, that the job of central cognition often ceases to exist. The internal representations the mind uses to guide actions may thus be best

understood as action-context-specific control struc-
tures rather than as passive recapitulations of external reality. The detailed, action-neutral inner models
that were to provide the domain for disembodied,
centralized cogitation stand revealed as slow, expensive, hard-to-maintain luxuries—top-end purchases
that cost-conscious nature will generally strive to
avoid.[10]

Because evolution favors efficiency, it makes sense that the
brain is part of a system that focuses on reducing energy output
and using whatever resources the world offers in order to promote efficiency and survival. As discussed earlier, making a process subconscious is nature's strategy for reducing energy and
increasing brain efficiency. When subconscious processing mod-
ules benefit survival, they become hardwired as part of the evolutionary process. Therefore it's far more accurate to view the brain
not as a kind of stand-alone computer, but as a uniquely important component of a broader system.

Systems thinking not only provides insights about nature's
design and the evolution of the brain; it greatly expands our creative opportunities for literally any design problem. New opportunities for sizable gains in efficiency can be achieved by actively
incorporating the environment as part of the solution instead of
passively accepting presumed, fixed constraints imposed by the
environment.

The incredible speed and maneuverability of the bluefin
tuna seems impossible when scientists examine the fish itself,
removed from its natural environment. But when scientists
observe the fish swimming, it becomes apparent that nature has
equipped this particular fish to exploit naturally occurring eddies
and vortices of its environment and also to gain additional speed
from the specialized interaction of its tail with the water.

It's examples like this that illustrate that nature has a propen-
sity for distributed solutions. This means that solutions involve

the relationship between the organism and its environment. Understanding complex ecosystems is not possible through a mindset that assumes that one individual object acts on another in a neat, linear cause-and-effect chain. Rather, complex systems in nature tend to emerge from simple rules that rely on decentralized, self-organizing interactions as well as feedback loops to yield efficient operation. This can be observed in ant colonies, beehives, termite mounds, and such.

Mitchel Resnick, an MIT-based leader in educating students about decentralized systems, has written:

> People seem to have a strong preference for centralization in almost everything they think and do. People tend to look for *the* cause, *the* reason, *the* driving force, *the* deciding factor. When people observe patterns and structures in the world (for example, the flocking patterns of birds or the foraging patterns of ants), they often assume centralized causes where none exist. And when people try to create patterns and structures in the world (for example, new organizations or new machines), they often impose centralized control where none is needed.[11]

Along this line of thinking, skilled lean managers of manufacturing plants tend to be skeptical of the need for highly sophisticated MRP (materials-requirements planning) software systems. MRP software basically keeps track of all the materials in a plant in order to schedule the work. Of course, when parts are not where the "centralized brain" expects them to be, employees make do with what is available. The alternative Toyota-style approach doesn't require a centralized brain, since lean processes are simplified and efficiently organized in order to pull needed materials from the next upstream process.

Interestingly, when a society's institutions evolve through a natural "evolutionary" process, rather than one of an imposed human design, the result tends to reflect decentralization and a selection of whatever works best. In describing the importance of knowledge communicated via a decentralized process of setting market prices, the Nobel laureate economist Friedrich Hayek emphasized that the "most significant fact about [market prices] is the economy of knowledge with which it operates, or how little the individual participants need to know in order to be able to take the right action."[12] It is difficult to overstate the wealth creation that has been and can be achieved from the utilization of market prices in a developed modern economy.

## Key points

- Because simplified, linear cause-and-effect analysis has proved so useful in our lives, we tend to apply it to components of a complex system while automatically assuming that improvement in a component will translate into improvement in the performance of the overall system. This may not be true—especially so when system components are highly dependent upon each other and when the improvement is made to a component that is not the key constraint impeding the system's performance.

- An overall systems view that focuses attention on relationships among components can reveal insights for potential changes that would not be discovered if one focused only on improving the local efficiencies of a system's individual components.

- The worldwide adoption of lean/theory-of-constraints thinking by manufacturing firms and, increasingly, by service firms is a testament to the usefulness of a systems-oriented worldview.

## CHAPTER 5

# HUMAN CONTROL SYSTEMS

To the extent that a scientific revolution represents a fundamental change in a discipline, the cognitive revolution in psychology was not particularly revolutionary. What changed least in this revolution was methodology. The experimental methods used in cognitive psychology are the same as those used in the behaviorism it overthrew. This methodological continuity results from the fact that both behaviorism and cognitive psychology are based on the same paradigm, which is also the basis of experimental psychology: the open-loop causal model of behavioral organization. A truly revolutionary approach to understanding the mind has been largely ignored because it is built on a paradigm that is inconsistent with conventional research methods. This new approach to psychology, called Perceptual Control Theory (PCT), is based on a closed-loop control model of behavioral organization that is tested using control engineering methods that are unfamiliar to most psychologists.

—Richard S. Marken
"You Say You Had a Revolution: Methodological
Foundations of Closed Loop Psychology"

Negative feedback control is not a new principle, but as far as the sciences of life are concerned it is an underutilized principle, mentioned by many but fully understood by few. Many people have suspected the existence of some such architecture, but the mainstream has never been willing to give up the causal model, at least not to an extent sufficient to encourage a major commitment of resources to the study of living hierarchically organized feedback control systems. Perhaps in this new millennium we will see a return to this basic concept, and finally an understanding of what it can mean to the sciences of life.

—William T. Powers
"The Neglected Phenomenon of
Negative Feedback Control"

## Core Belief 4:
## Behavior is control of perception

The big idea in this chapter is that a paradigm shift is slowly taking place in the social sciences regarding how we think about human behavior. The new thinking can be summarized as follows:

Core Belief 4: Human behavior is purposeful, so it can be productively analyzed as a living control system that acts to maintain the perceptions of important variables as close as possible to preferred levels. In short, behavior is control of perception. A control perspective reveals the underlying weakness in viewing the world primarily as stimulus-response experiences.

Put simply, life is about a continual process of controlling—or trying to control—our experiences. That is, we compare our actual experiences to our preferred experiences and, as needed, we take action to get our experiences to match what we want. The difference between what we want and our actual experience is labeled error. Hence, control is a process of reducing error. When we put on a coat before going outside, that we're acting to control our body temperature is an easily understood concept. Much less obvious is that this same control process continuously drives our behavior. It is a ubiquitous and essentially invisible feature of our daily lives.

A control viewpoint shifts our attention from what a person is doing to a person's goals and their perceptions of variables related to achieving those goals. Note that a changing context can easily lead to different actions to achieve goals. So, to understand behavior we need to view a person from the inside out and concern ourselves with their control variables, the ones that are essential for them to get what they want. The key point is that when we know a person's goal, we usually can predict the consequences of their actions although we may not be able to predict the actions taken.

Non-living things are ideally suited to be studied using the linear cause-and-effect/stimulus-response lens. Using this method of looking at the world, researchers in the hard sciences—physics, chemistry, and the like—have produced astounding gains in our knowledge about how the world works. However, a paradigm shift has been under way in understanding human behavior based on the fact that living organisms function as control systems. Simple linear cause-and-effect analysis masks the fundamental operation of a control system; when applied to human behavior, it can easily result in illusory research findings.

In addition to being a part of living organisms, control systems are built into various mechanical and electronic devices. Here's an example of a control system: on a cold winter's day, you open a window in your living room (cause or stimulus) and soon observe that hot air is flowing from the room vents (effect or response). If you were unaware of the existence and role of the thermostat, you might believe that opening the window *caused* the furnace to send out heat. But that belief, which offers the illusion of understanding the situation, would be superficial. Rather, there is a control system at work in which the thermostat has a reference setting, a desired room temperature, and a sensor that senses room temperature. The thermostat–furnace-room system functions as a closed loop in which the current room temperature is compared to the reference setting and a difference or error, a temperature lower than the one set, turns the furnace on to deliver heated air, which in turn increases the room temperature, and so it goes. Put another way, stimulus *affects* response and response *affects* stimulus.[1] This is much different from an open-loop situation such as a billiard ball hitting (cause) another ball, which then moves (effect).

## Perceptual Control Theory (PCT)

Perception is the way our brain experiences the world. What you perceive is not the object "out there"; instead, you're receiving a set of neural signals that your brain utilizes to "serve up" a representation of the object.

Living organisms have purposes: to control the variables that are important to them. They behave so that their perception of a controlled variable moves closer to their reference setting for that variable. A comprehensive treatment of this idea—one that employs a *hierarchical* organization of control systems using the mechanism of negative feedback control—has been developed by William T. Powers and is called Perceptual Control Theory (PCT). In commenting on Powers's classic book *Behavior: The Control of Perception,* first published in 1973, Russell Ackoff noted:

> [It] is, in my opinion, a major event in the development of the psychology of perception. The completely new approach he has developed using cybernetic concepts cannot help but be seminal, instigating a new and important line of investigation

of a wide range of psychological phenomena in addition to perception. His new way of looking at and conceptualizing old things will help to open the way for a series of important discoveries, and these—because of the rigorous framework he provides—are likely to be sounder scientifically than most of the earlier work that they will displace.[2]

Furthermore, Thomas Kuhn, famous for his explanation of paradigm shifts in science, commented about how exciting the book's PCT framework is and that he would "be watching with interest what happens to research in the directions in which Powers points." What did happen? Certainly not a fast paradigm shift, but instead there has been slow progress over the last forty years, with more and more attention given to PCT principles in a wide variety of research areas.[3]

If you don't know the variable a person is working at controlling, or its reference setting, it would be easy to observe his or her actions and then come to a wrong conclusion about what the person really is doing. Consider again the furnace scenario. If the thermostat was set to a very low temperature, the action of opening a window would not promptly be followed by a rush of hot air from the vents. That would then be called an "outlier" event by those who had previously documented the cause-effect relationship between window opening and hot air flowing. But for those who are aware of the actual control system in operation, this situation is completely understandable—and predictable.

Why have the social sciences, such as psychology, downplayed the phenomenon of control? The answer is that we tend not to pay attention to that which cannot be directly observed—that is, to the controlled variables. Instead, we observe, say, people's actions that seem to be in response to external causes in the environment and we tend to automatically view these as straightforward cause and effect in operation.

Moreover, for a long time the scientific method of linear cause and effect as practiced in the hard sciences has been the dominant methodology practiced in the social sciences as well. Statistical studies that measure the correlation between independent and dependent variables have been the standard means by which empirical research articles are accepted for publication in academic journals. In contrast, PCT involves especially difficult challenges for researchers in doing empirical work focused on control variables. It requires a methodology to identify and work with control variables—a radical departure from standard statistical methods.

The impact of PCT on the social sciences in general, and on business and economics in particular, appears to be in a very early stage. Once I "got it" as to how living control systems operate, I became skeptical of both studies and management programs that involve incentives without any regard for the higher-level goals of employees. Absent an appreciation for a hierarchical control system, managements' experiments with a variety of carrots and sticks are of dubious value in terms of long-term employee productivity and job satisfaction. A refreshingly different angle that ties into higher-level employee goals is presented by Daniel Pink in his book *Drive: The Surprising Truth about What Motivates Us*. Pink makes a persuasive case that managements should tie into three elements of true motivation: autonomy, mastery, and purpose.[4]

## Change and stability

In the 1800s, the French physiologist Claude Bernard noted that the stability of an organism's internal environment is the means for living in an environment of varying conditions.[5] His conceptual insight later evolved into the understanding of homeostatic control systems, which use a sensor, a comparator that includes a desired range for the sensed variable, and an effector to act on the environment.

In his classic book *The Principles of Psychology*, published in 1890, the psychologist William James expanded Bernard's insight by generalizing it to describe human behavior as the use of variable means to attain constant ends. He illustrated the distinction between non-living things and living organisms with two examples.

> If some iron filings be sprinkled on a table and a magnet brought near them, they will fly through the air for a certain distance and stick to its surface.... But let a card cover the poles of the magnet, and the filings will press forever against [the card's] surface without its ever occurring to them to pass around its sides.

> If we now pass from such actions as these to those of living things, we notice a striking difference. Romeo wants Juliet as the filings want the magnet; and if no obstacles intervene, he moves towards her by as straight a line as they. But Romeo and Juliet, if a wall be built between them, do not remain idiotically pressing their faces against its opposite sides like the magnet and the filings with the card. Romeo soon finds a circuitous way, by scaling the wall or otherwise, of touching Juliet's lips directly. With the filings the path is fixed; whether it reaches the end depends on accidents. With the lover it is the end which is fixed, the path may be modified indefinitely.[6]

Although this concept of maintaining control was later formalized and expanded by developments in engineering control systems, mainstream psychology kept on using the stimulus-response mindset, which was based on linear cause and effect, for understanding behavior.

Maintaining control is one side of the survival coin; changing to gain efficiency is the other. It's common knowledge that evolution favors mechanisms that efficiently promote the survival and improvement of an organism's overall functioning. Negative feedback control is all about efficiency.[7] It is the heart of any control system, and its extraordinary usefulness was discovered by engineers and put to use in the design of machines. The basic idea was neatly illustrated by the development of James Watt's flyball governor during the Industrial Revolution (see Figure 5.1). The problem then was to maintain a nearly constant speed for a steam engine even though speed was sensitive to boiler pressure as well as to the workload placed on the steam engine.

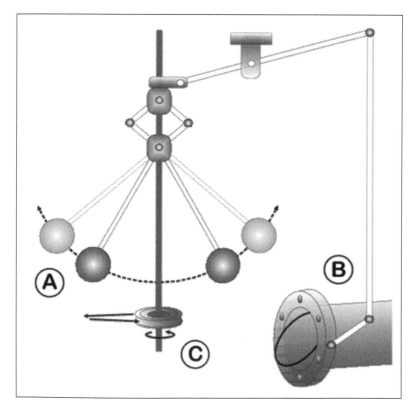

**Figure 5.1 Watt's Governor**

Here we see a mechanical application of negative feedback control. Power from the steam engine is supplied to the governor through a belt connected to the lower wheel. In this example of a surge in speed, we observe at point "A" that the increased speed causes the flyballs to move outward from the rotating shaft. The outward movement of the flyballs in turn moves the mechanical lever that causes the throttle valve to reduce steam flow ("B"). In a lower throttle position, steam flow is reduced, with the result that engine speed slows back down to the setpoint ("C"). Consequently, the steam engine's speed remains steady in spite of fluctuating steam pressure and workload. Note the efficiency that is gained by using negative feedback control. No human operator needs to manually take action to adjust a steam valve and/or adjust the amount of heat supplied to the boiler.

A control system controls what it senses—what it perceives. Controlling means producing repeatable consequences through variable actions. As emphasized by Powers, we vary our behavior in order to control perceptions that matter to us: behavior is control of perception. Powers built upon the fact that we never experience physical reality directly but rather that what we see, hear, touch, and smell is composed of neural signals. He proposed a pyramid or hierarchy of control systems within which higher-level systems send their output to lower-level systems. Higher-order goals do not impact behavior directly but set the perceptual standards for lower-order systems. The goal of a higher-level system is translated into a reference signal for a comparator, which is a part of a lower-level system, as shown in Figure 5.2 in a diagram that focuses on a single controlled variable operating at the lowest level of the hierarchy.

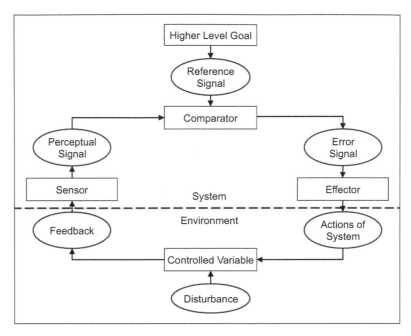

**Figure 5.2 Components of a Control System**

Lower-level systems work much faster than higher-level systems because they involve shorter neural pathways and less-complex processing than do higher-level systems. In fact, for a hierarchical control system to be stable, the higher-level systems necessarily must be slower than the lower-level systems. Reference signals set by higher, slower systems communicate to lower systems not what actions to take but rather what to perceive. At the lowest level of the hierarchy, we find sensors, such as our eyes, that perceive aspects of the external environment that are relayed as neural signals, and effectors that receive neural signals that direct our muscles to take actions on the external environment.[8]

Note the feedback loop at work in which a disturbance in the environment impacts a controlled variable. The difference between the perception of the controlled variable and its reference signal results in the comparator sending an error signal. This, in turn, causes actions to counteract the disturbance in order to reduce the error. Thus there is a loop in which what we perceive affects our actions and our actions affect what we perceive. PCT encourages us to shift from a stimulus-response way of seeing the world to an awareness that we act to oppose disturbances to controlled variables.

When we're driving a car we encounter a multitude of external environmental disturbances impacting the car. Without attempting to, or needing to, compute explicitly the appropriate actions to deal with each of these disturbances, we automatically sense both the position of our car relative to the middle-lane marker as well as our car's speed and we make continuous and fast adjustments to reduce error as depicted in Figure 5.2. A driver turns the car in a direction that matches a higher-level goal, such as arriving at work on time. That goal was set by an even higher goal of performing well at work in order to continue earning a paycheck and hopefully getting promoted. That goal in turn was set by an even higher goal of being a responsible wife or husband. Note that answers to "why" questions are found by moving up the hierarchy, and answers to "how" questions are found by moving down.

Keep in mind that my description of PCT in this chapter is extremely abbreviated. In an endnote to this chapter, I list recommended readings and websites to visit that cover important topics that are not discussed here.[9] Some of these topics include computer experiments that demonstrate how one's behavior in achieving goals under varying environmental disturbances is explained via PCT; Powers's hypothesized levels of our hierarchical control systems; the mathematics of building PCT models; testing for the existence of controlled variables; "moving up a level" in the hierarchy of control to resolve lower-level conflict situations; and a variety of technical topics such as the reorganization of our hierarchical control systems—that is, learning.[10]

That our behavior is fundamentally about controlling our perceptions is an idea of significant importance. But remember that it is just one of the four core beliefs. Ideally, all the core beliefs work in tandem to improve one's worldview and help one deal with important challenges.

## Key points

- Perception is how our mind experiences the world. What we perceive affects what we do and what we do affects what we perceive.
- In contrast to non-living things, living organisms have purposes. We behave in ways to keep our perceptions of important variables—our goals—close to where we want them to be. Behavior is control of perception.
- If we disregard control variables, we can falsely conclude that we know what a person is doing by simply observing his or her actions.
- Negative feedback control is pervasive in living organisms, and is a means by which to efficiently orchestrate actions to achieve desired perceptions.
- Perceptual Control Theory (PCT) helps us as humans—with our "bundled" body and brain—to understand how we function as hierarchically organized control systems. Higher levels set goals for lower levels by sending reference signals, perceptual goals.
- When people working together have sharply different high-level goals, conflict is to be expected. When their high-level goals are similar, expect cooperation.
- We improve our worldviews by understanding human behavior from the inside out: by acknowledging that people have goals and take actions in order to control their environment in ways that enable them to achieve their goals. This way of thinking avoids seemingly plausible but perhaps flat-out misleading conclusions that the cause of what a person is doing is merely a response to a stimulus in the external environment.

# CHAPTER 6

# A CASE STUDY: FREE TO CHOOSE MEDICINE

[T]he single most powerful explanation for how the FDA works is ... the bureaucratic imperative that seeks to expand turf no matter what its consequences for others.

—Richard A. Epstein
*Overdose: How Excessive Government Regulation*
*Stifles Pharmaceutical Innovation*

The way the FDA now behaves, and the adverse consequences, are not an accident, not a result of some easily corrected human mistake, but a consequence of its constitution in precisely the same way that a meow is related to the constitution of a cat.

—Milton and Rose Friedman
*Free To Choose: A Personal Statement*

## Different worldviews

This chapter briefly outlines the proposal that is treated comprehensively in my book *Free To Choose Medicine: Better Drugs Sooner at Lower Cost* (a third edition is in progress for publication in 2015). I argue that we need a major shift in how we think about the current drugs-to-patients system in the United States.[1] In analyzing the reasons in support of this proposal as well as the counterarguments by those opposed, you'll see how different worldviews can lead to different conclusions. In general, a deeper understanding of the worldviews held by those who disagree with your position can suggest how to overcome obstacles. You can alter your use of language, for example, or solicit feedback in order to reach common ground.

As has been discussed, the strong pull of our worldviews helps or hinders us in dealing with complex problems—including the volatile issue of access to new medical treatments. In this regard, the famous physicist Richard Feynman noted, "The first principle is that you must not fool yourself and you are the easiest person to fool."

As an example, consider the editors and reviewers of highly rated academic journals. As the guardians of scientific knowledge, surely they view the world (and the papers submitted to them) with the utmost skepticism about the validity of experimental results. You might be surprised as to their susceptibility for being fooled.

In 2010, Professor Diederik Stapel was appointed dean of Tilburg University's School of Social and Behavioral Sciences in the Netherlands. Shortly thereafter, Stapel's reputation transitioned from that of a highly regarded professor with extensively published articles in prestigious academic journals to the biggest con man in academic science. He had authored at least fifty-five fraudulent articles.[2]

When the fraud became public knowledge, many pointed out how "obvious" was the artificial data that Stapel used in his articles. But the more interesting point is how clever he was in understanding how the world occurred to editors and reviewers. The papers describing his "experiments" were written in a way that was especially appealing to them. In an interview after the fraud was made public, he explained how his experimental designs were closely tied to the existing body of knowledge, which included research that had been personally contributed by the editors and reviewers. They perceived his experiments as logical extensions of their work, the next steps forward, that mainstream thinking should take. All this misdirection was wrapped in an elegant and simple presentation style that further convinced the editors and reviewers that he was delivering genuine insights.

## Personal freedom

The important takeaway here is to recognize that we are all primed to perceive situations in ways that are consistent with our own personal worldviews. In the rest of this chapter, I'll offer reasons for you to question the current and widely accepted view that the absolute control and monopoly over access to new drugs by the Food and Drug Administration (FDA) is a requirement in order for us to have what it deems safe and effective drugs. It is my strong belief that we're being fooled if we blindly accept this view.

Let's look at one situation where the heavy hand of status-quo FDA regulatory processes resulted in every parent's worst nightmare: the death of a son or daughter after being unable to access a new, not-yet-FDA-approved drug that doctors consider to be the best chance to save your child's life. Such a nightmare situation may not have hit your family. And because the news media rarely report this issue, you may well be unaware of the extent of the problem: the loss of your personal freedom to choose medicine. Make no mistake, what we actually have on our hands is an invisible graveyard of patients who were, are, and will be denied timely access to potentially lifesaving medical treatments.

A good friend of mine, Frank Burroughs, lost his daughter Abigail to cancer when she was twenty-one. During a speech she gave at her high-school graduation, she remarked, "Success is fleeting, but when all is said and done, all you have is your character." By any measure, Abigail was a remarkable young woman.

On two separate occasions she failed to meet the FDA's strict requirements for enrollment in a clinical trial in which she might have been treated with a new, not-yet-FDA-approved drug, Erbitux. Her highly respected oncologist believed that this new drug had real potential to save her life. Erbitux was later approved by the FDA—but too late for Abigail.

Many who have had the experience of losing a family member after being unable to access a new drug that showed potential to be the best medical treatment are outraged at their loss of personal freedom. They feel helpless to do anything about it. Not Frank. He founded the Abigail Alliance for Better Access to Developmental Drugs to help those on death's doorstep to possibly gain faster access to innovative new drugs—access his own daughter did not get.

The Abigail Alliance represents a patient-advocate worldview that affirms patients' right to access medical treatments that they and their doctors believe offer the best chance to improve health or even save lives. In sharp contrast, the FDA primarily represents a worldview that asserts that the cost of delayed access incurred by today's patients is a requirement in order that patients in the future have what it deems safe and effective drugs.

## Language and systems thinking

Earlier chapters emphasized the benefits from our paying attention to critical assumptions—often camouflaged, rather than clarified, by language—and to using a systems view when grappling with complex problems. This advice is particularly relevant for gaining a deeper understanding of the FDA's current monopoly on access to new drugs. By gaining this understanding, we can see through the alarming reports from the news media about approved drugs—reports that invariably call for even stronger FDA control so as to presumably avoid any unexpected adverse side effects in the future. While this may sound logical on the surface, it's merely the automatic result of a flawed worldview.

Let's dig deeper using a systems-thinking worldview that's attuned to the core beliefs described in prior chapters. The starting point is to be absolutely clear about the stated goal of the drugs-to-patients system in which the FDA regulatory process is the major component. That goal should be better drugs (and other medical treatments), sooner, at lower cost. However, a so-called goal of offering safe and effective drugs ignores two other critical objectives: (1) reducing the time from drug discovery to patient use and (2) lowering the cost of drugs.

Over the last half century, the cost of therapeutic drugs has been on a steep upward trajectory due to relentless demands from the FDA for ever more extensive clinical trials. Patient-advocate organizations, such as the Abigail Alliance, continually point out the needless suffering and deaths that result from delayed access.[3] Contributing to the problem is the early abandonment of new drugs that have huge potential to significantly improve the standard of care for serious illnesses.

Why, then, are they abandoned? Because investment capital tends to go elsewhere when economic costs are large and the potential rewards are both uncertain and in the distant future. In particular, a huge roadblock exists for venture capitalists to fund start-up biotech companies that have radically different (non-mainstream) ways to treat diseases. That roadblock is the substantial uncertainty about future FDA statistical and clinical testing milestones. A radically different new drug will kick the FDA's cautious mentality into high gear, regardless of potential patient benefits. And no one can predict what the FDA's clinical testing requirements for such drugs will be like in the distant future. As business risk significantly increases, investors back away from committing investment capital. This is one practical example of how the FDA's focus on optimizing local efficiency—that of clinical testing—works to the detriment of achieving the system goal of better drugs, sooner, at lower cost. Achieving the system goal depends upon substantial, early-stage R&D investments that can lead to breakthrough new medical treatments.

How did the FDA become such a slow, inefficient bureaucracy? The answer concerns the agency's culture and is in two parts.

First, any government agency, such as the FDA, the Environmental Protection Agency, or the Department of Energy, has a historically demonstrated motivation to expand its bureaucratic turf through passing more and more regulations. Second, if the FDA approves a drug that later causes an unexpectedly high occurrence of serious adverse side effects, including deaths, the news media, the public, and Congress blame the FDA for not "doing its job." On the other hand, inexcusably long delays in reviewing clinical trial data and new drug applications, or inappropriately rejecting a new drug that could save lives, goes unnoticed by the news media. It's no surprise, then, that the FDA has very potent incentives to "err on the side of caution." In practice, this deadly overcaution keeps in motion its relentless demand for more extensive testing, which is enormously expensive in both time and money.

In terms of Perceptual Control Theory as discussed in Chapter 5, we can understand, and predict, FDA behavior primarily because of its management acting in ways to minimize—that is, control—negative publicity about adverse side effects from approved drugs. The cost of delayed access to innovative new drugs almost never causes a problem for the FDA. Perhaps the sole exception was the HIV/AIDS activists during the 1980s and 1990s, who literally camped outside the agency's offices in Washington and caused such embarrassment to the FDA that eventually HIV/AIDS drugs gained expedited approval.

Let's return to those seemingly simple words: "safe and effective." Upon closer examination, "safe" is an especially fuzzy concept that misleads people into believing that all drugs can be neatly classified as either safe or unsafe. Recall from Chapter 3 the point that we tend to view the world through a lens of simplified and objectified noun concepts that cover up what are actually dynamic, context-sensitive processes. Safety is, in fact, context-dependent. For example, aspirin, while generally regarded as quite benign, can be lethal for elderly patients with stomach problems. Those faced with life-threatening illnesses surely are less concerned about a drug's safety profile and more about its potential to extend their lives. So the attributes of a drug, such as its safety and effectiveness, are inextricably involved with an individual patient's condition and his or her preference for risk versus potential health improvement.

As for effectiveness, the FDA process for determining if a drug is effective rests with blind, randomized control trials that use a carefully screened group of patients. A drug is tested to determine if the average treatment result exceeds specific FDA statistical milestones. The FDA's focus on the average patient makes it much easier for the FDA to make decisions about whether a drug is effective or not. But the result is a one-size-fits-all regulatory straitjacket that can easily reject a drug that does not exceed statistical milestones but that is, in fact, effective for one or more subgroups of patients and/or effective when used in combination with another drug.

Twenty-first-century medicine is all about molecular science, which enables drug developers to design drugs for targeted patients based on an individual patient's genetic makeup and biomarkers. (A biomarker is a laboratory measurement that reflects the activity of a disease process.) An ideal personalized medicine system would combine high-powered molecular science and information technology that enables fast-paced learning and the sharing of data; this, however, is diametrically opposite from the FDA's rigid clinical-trial methodology.

In his book *The Cure in the Code: How 20th Century Law Is Undermining 21st Century Medicine,* Peter Huber emphasizes that

> [m]edicine's ability to generate torrents of data that are relevant to a drug's performance is expanding far faster than Washington's ability to make sense of it all.... By retreating into the dark comfort of blinded trials that track clinical symptoms, the FDA solves the complexity problem by refusing to get mired in molecular details—the details on which the progress of the disease and the efficacy and safety of targeted drugs actually hinge.
>
> Legislation enacted in 2012 attempts to yet again nudge the FDA back to the future—but once more leaves it all to the agency's discretion.[4]

Note the key phrase "but once more leaves it all to the agency's discretion."

The solution, I believe, to these problems is the Free To Choose Medicine proposal. It's unique in that it would bring external competition to the FDA's regulatory process and most certainly would not leave it all to the agency's discretion.

## Consumer choice and competition

The drugs-to-patients system begins with laboratory research, which includes in vitro analyses and animal testing. After a drug developer selects a promising new drug for submission to the FDA, a three-step series of human clinical trials begins.

- In Phase I, a small number (generally in the range of 20 to 100) of healthy volunteers are given the drug in increasingly large doses to judge a safe level of exposure.
- In Phase II, a larger number (typically from 100 to 500) of patients with the actual disease being studied are given the

drug to further evaluate safety and to establish an effective dosage level.

- In Phase III, randomized control trials generally involve 1,000 to 5,000 patients, roughly half of whom receive the new drug, while the other half receive either a placebo or the current standard treatment for the disease.

The time to gain permission to run each of the three phases, and to complete the multiple clinical trials involved, plus the time for the FDA to make a yes-or-no approval decision on the developer's New Drug Application (NDA), can easily exceed ten years. About one in twelve drugs that start clinical trials eventually receives FDA approval. As such, the total accumulated cost for securing one new drug approval is, on average, well in excess of a billion dollars. It's not surprising that the costs of prescription drugs have skyrocketed. But it doesn't have to be this way.

With a systems-thinking worldview, I find it plausible to conclude that the FDA itself is the key constraint to achieving the system goal of better drugs, sooner, at lower cost. Instead of automatically assuming that centralized FDA control is necessary, a systems perspective focuses on how all the parts work together. I believe we should consider the potential improvement in achieving the goal of better drugs, sooner, at lower cost by using consumer choice and competition—elements that are notably absent from the FDA's monopoly on access to new drugs.

Those of us old enough will remember the AT&T phone monopoly that gave us clunky rotary-dial telephones. Our only choice then was what color phone to buy. After AT&T's monopoly was broken, telecommunication innovation was turbocharged, consumer choice flourished, and firms competed to deliver innovative cell phones that consumers greatly appreciate. Another example is FedEx. Competition from FedEx's guaranteed one-day delivery of packages compelled the government's postal service to respond and also offer one-day mail delivery. Imagine the health benefits if the drugs-to-patients system followed a similar competitive path. This is not a hypothetical, impractical notion. Consumer choice and competition work to the ultimate benefit of consumers.

However, permitting a competitive alternative to the FDA's regulatory process is strikingly inconsistent with FDA proponents' "safe and effective" worldview. They have great difficulty in even entertaining the thought of breaking the FDA's monopoly. Their answer is to rely on legislation that always sounds very impressive, but changes little of the structure of the existing system. At various times legislation has been passed to accelerate the approval process; ironically enough, however, the FDA has control of the crafting of regulations that implement the legislation.

Patient-advocate organizations like the Abigail Alliance have argued that the FDA can easily become motivated to slow down the implementation of accelerated approval legislation due to its concern about a reduction in randomized control trial data and about negative publicity resulting from adverse side effects from drugs that might receive accelerated approval. Can we realistically expect any government bureaucracy to restructure itself and voluntarily reduce its monopolistic power? Personally, I'm doubtful.

The FDA's power is on full display with its requirement for randomized control trials that greatly facilitate its statistical analyses for approval decisions, while providing a scientific shield to defend its decisions. A strong case can be made that the FDA urgently needs to transition away from conventional randomized control trials and employ adaptive clinical trials, which facilitate adjustments to testing procedures based on learning during a trial about a drug's safety and efficacy for different subpopulations.

The real issue here is the undisturbed power of a monopolistic organization to innovate (or not) at its own pace, all the while maintaining the organization's business-as-usual culture. If AT&T had maintained its monopoly, the pace of innovation in telecommunications in general, and personal phone technology in particular, could well have been an order of magnitude slower.

Apple, Samsung, Motorola, and other innovative companies would have been kept on the bench—good for AT&T, but bad for consumers. The economist William Baumol noted that in a free-market competitive environment, fast-paced innovation is a "matter of life and death" for firms. A fast-paced, innovative environment for the drugs-to-patients system is literally a matter of life and death for patients dealing with serious diseases.

In theory, the FDA's existing "compassionate use" program for patients like Abigail Burroughs addresses the glaring need for access to not-yet-approved drugs. In practice, it rarely works because the FDA doesn't want patients to circumvent the randomized control-trial enrollment process. Doctors have described the procedure to obtain a compassionate-use exemption for their patients as agonizingly similar to an IRS audit.

## Free To Choose Medicine: better drugs, sooner, at lower cost

In contrast, Free To Choose Medicine is a practical way to implement freedom of choice. This is illustrated in Figure 6.1. After a demonstration of safety and preliminary efficacy by completion of Phase I trials and one or more Phase II trials, drug developers would have three options. First, they could continue on the standard clinical-trial track. Second, they could request to put their new drug on the Free To Choose track that would enable patients, advised by their doctors, to make an informed decision about using the new drug. Third, they could elect to proceed on the standard FDA track and concurrently request to be put on the Free To Choose track.

The operational details of the dual-track system are fully presented and explained in the second edition of my book *Free To Choose Medicine: Better Drugs Sooner at Lower Cost*. This proposal includes limited-liability waivers so that patients can voluntarily accept responsibility for the risks of Free To Choose drugs. Also included is a discussion of the role of an advisory committee to determine if a drug is suitable to be put on the Free To Choose track as well as if and when a drug should be pulled for safety concerns.

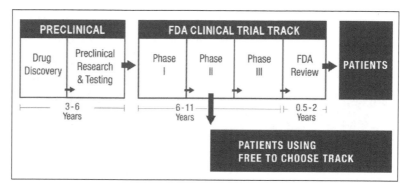

**Figure 6.1  Free To Choose Track Option**

The heart of the dual-track system is the aggregating and sharing of information by means of the Tradeoff Evaluation Drug Database (TEDD) as displayed in Figure 6.2.

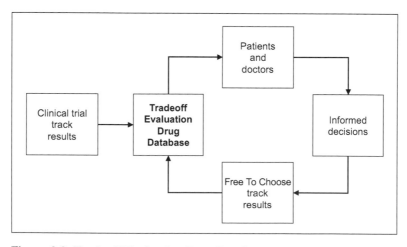

**Figure 6.2  Tradeoff Evaluation Drug Database**

Information on TEDD would be made available to the public through a government-supervised website. This would include drug treatment results from clinical trials as well as doctor-supplied data on Free To Choose drugs. The doctor-supplied data would focus on patient health details including genetic makeup, treatment results, and relevant biomarker data. In this manner, patients and their doctors can obtain the information they need to evaluate a drug's potential benefits versus risks so they can make informed decisions about whether or not to use a Free To Choose drug.

In order to prevent Free To Choose Medicine from being undermined by an overly turf-protective FDA, the TEDD and other Free To Choose track functions would need to be operated by a separate but still competent authority such as the National Institutes of Health.

The key issue is: are we and our doctors competent enough to make decisions about the use of not-yet-FDA-approved drugs? The FDA and those relying on a "safe and effective" worldview contend we are not. According to them, the FDA must tightly control both access to, and information about, not-yet-approved drugs. Interestingly, even without TEDD's insightful and up-to-date information-sharing, the Abigail Alliance has fought for early access to nineteen new drugs it viewed as especially promising for life-threatening diseases. All nineteen were eventually approved by the FDA.[5]

The primary benefit to patients of Free To Choose Medicine is fast access to the most innovative new drugs that show exceptional early efficacy in treating serious diseases. For example, if you suffer from ALS—amyotrophic lateral sclerosis, commonly known as Lou Gehrig's disease—you will most likely die a horribly painful death in the near future. You simply cannot wait five or more years for FDA approval of a drug that in early Phase II clinical trials shows real potential to extend or even save the lives of ALS patients. Joshua Boger, founder of Vertex Pharmaceuticals, adds:

In my experience, drugs that do not work and drugs that substantially exceed minimal expectations are easy to spot. While there are exceptions, if you need a statistician to measure benefit in Phase II, then the drug didn't work that well. In a world of profound opportunity to change medicine, maybe we shouldn't be working on those middling cases. Identify as fast as possible the drugs that don't work (and learn from them), and identify as fast as possible the upside surprises.[6]

Those relying on a "safe and effective" worldview appear to underappreciate three key issues. First, the Information Age, with its widespread Internet availability, provides the capability to deliver highly useful data that equips doctors and their patients to become much better decision-makers. Second, as long as their names are kept confidential, people are generally very motivated to share their personal health data in order to advance research and help their own medical situation. Third, widespread data-sharing enables innovation to flourish in ways that central planners are unable to forecast. It is noteworthy that during the last half century, molecular science and information technology have achieved no less than revolutionary progress, yet the FDA's clinical testing methodology has changed very little.

In Chapter 4 the point was made that complex systems in nature tend to rely on decentralized interactions and feedback to yield high productivity (e.g., ant colonies, beehives, termite mounds, and the like). In a similar vein, Free To Choose Medicine would provide open access to currently confidential information about clinical trial results as well as create new information about Free To Choose track patients and their treatment results. All this uniquely valuable, decentralized information would then be used in a feedback loop that is orchestrated by accessing TEDD.

## Observational data

Improving health by using decentralized data is not a new idea. What *is* new is the capability of Free To Choose Medicine to leverage decentralized data to deliver extraordinary performance gains for the entire drugs-to-patients system. The exponential growth in recent years of websites that enable patients to share medical information, such as www.PatientsLikeMe.com, is a strong indicator that TEDD would be used extensively. TEDD's compilation of Free To Choose track drug results would be referred to as observational data, in contrast to data from randomized control trials.

One certainly must acknowledge the power of data from well-designed, randomized control trials for scientific, cause-and-effect analysis. But the systems-thinking worldview informs us that learning is a complex process that occurs in both controlled as well as uncontrolled environments. Much of the current practice of medicine was adopted without the benefit of randomized trials. Most studies of surgical procedures are based solely on retrospective analyses of practices that were adopted by trial and error. Moreover, consider off-label drug use, in which an FDA-approved drug is prescribed for a condition for which it was not FDA tested or approved. Observational data about off-label treatment results is shared and communicated via private-sector organizations. Off-label drug use is a window into an environment where doctors use their skills and in-depth patient knowledge to experiment and develop drug treatments that can provide enormous benefits to patients.

In some ways, Free To Choose Medicine would be quite similar to off-label use, as both involve decentralized learning from individualized experimentation with drugs that have passed through basic clinical safety testing. However, because TEDD would collect many—possibly thousands or tens of thousands—individual experiences with particular drugs and aggregate them in a way that makes direct comparison to approved drugs possible, it would be vastly superior to off-label use.

Ideally, Free To Choose Medicine legislation would empower the FDA, based on results posted on TEDD, to grant observational approval that complements its standard approval. Status-quo proponents may well point out that this new approval mechanism accepts a lower scientific standard than the so-called gold standard of randomized control trials. They may claim that it will undermine enrollment in randomized control trials. If doctors strongly believe that a new, experimental drug is clearly the best choice for their patients, then forcing patients to take a chance on receiving a placebo or an inferior drug in a clinical trial is plainly unethical. Free To Choose Medicine would, in fact, interfere with enrollment in unethical trials; but it would not interfere with randomized control trial enrollment for ethical trials in which knowledgeable doctors are genuinely uncertain about the relative efficacy of an experimental drug. The bottom line is that randomized control trials make the FDA's decision-making easier. That patients should suffer and die without a choice of medical treatment in order that some people have an easier time at their jobs is equal parts tragedy and outrage.

As a practical matter, approved drugs based on randomized control trials have subsequently yielded unexpected adverse side effects, including deaths, because the real-world population of patients using the drug has widely different health conditions compared to the narrow, homogeneous population of patients who are tested with a drug in randomized control trials. The advantage of TEDD's observational data is that as a Free To Choose drug shows effectiveness and safety, more patients will use it. If favorable treatment results continue, even more patients will use it. Consequently, for a drug that is especially effective, the number of Free To Choose patients should be overwhelmingly larger than any randomized control trial population. This size advantage would compensate for observational data's lack of strict randomization. Conversely, a Free To Choose drug that does not perform well would see little increased usage over time and most likely a sharp decline in usage. This is a self-adjusting system that relies on consumer choice. TEDD's observational data would lead to fast-paced learning about treatment results for various subpopulations. This kind of learning not only informs doctors so they can better treat existing patients but also improves the R&D decisions of biopharmaceutical companies to the benefit of future patients.

## The benefits of a dynamic, self-adjusting system

What is meant by "free to choose"? Here, personal freedom implies the power to act to achieve a purpose while not harming others. For such freedom to thrive, a society's culture must value the feedback observed in the consequences of the individual's actions so that knowledge improves over time, thereby creating new opportunities for even more informed choices.

A preference for consumers to have freedom of choice instead of bureaucratic control is consistent with this meaning of freedom. However, the proposed breaking of the FDA's monopoly is not based solely on an argument for more individual freedom and less government control as a simple matter of principle. While of the utmost importance, freedom is but one component of a larger system.

We need the drugs-to-patients system to adapt quickly to our ever-changing technological environment. A very reasonable forecast is that the future will bring an accelerating pace in medical innovation, coupled with the widespread advancement of personalized medicine. Diagnostic testing will match patients according to their genetic makeup with drugs that are much more likely to work for them and have fewer adverse side effects. In this kind of environment, early access will become more and more beneficial over time. The significance of Free To Choose Medicine is that it would permit early access and dramatically speed up the delivery of medical advancements. Attesting to the common sense evident in the principles of Free To Choose Medicine, former FDA commissioner Andrew von Eschenbach points out:

> Breakthrough technologies deserve a breakthrough in the way the FDA evaluates them. Take regenerative medicine. If a company can grow cells that repair the retina in a lab, patients who've been blinded by macular degeneration shouldn't have to wait years while the FDA asks the company to complete laborious clinical trials proving efficacy. Instead, after proof of concept and safety testing, the product could be approved for marketing with every eligible patient entered in a registry so the company and the FDA can establish efficacy through post-market studies.[7]

On the Free To Choose track, a new drug that shows strong positive results, as noted earlier, would lead to a surge in use by patients with diverse characteristics that more accurately reflect the general patient population of users. Consequently, the new drug would have an even more reliable safety profile after FDA approval.

It should not be shocking that a decade-long (or more) clinical testing and approval process with a tab of over a billion dollars leads to very high prescription prices set by drug companies striving to achieve a satisfactory return on their investment (ROI). Free To Choose Medicine addresses that problem directly through competitive pressure and reduced regulatory costs. It should not be surprising that drug developers invest with expectations for achieving a satisfactory ROI commensurate with the risk they are taking. The higher the expenditures for clinical testing, and the longer it takes for drug revenues to be realized, the lower the ROI.

Lower drug prices can be achieved in two ways: (1) change the environment so that drug companies can achieve the same level of ROI with lower prescription drug prices, and (2) promote greater competition among drug companies. With Free To Choose Medicine, both can be achieved.

If Free To Choose Medicine becomes a reality, drug development firms would receive revenue sooner from the sale of drugs through the Free To Choose track. Raising capital in advance of any FDA approval would be far easier if TEDD data for a firm's new drug showed strong positive results. In addition, information accessible through TEDD about Free To Choose drugs would lead to increased efficiency of biopharmaceutical research and development outlays; there would be faster and more accurate decisions about which new drug programs to shut down and which to accelerate. Consumer choice would spur innovation and competition not only for drug companies, but also for the FDA.

The biggest reduction in prescription drug prices would most likely follow from the plain evidence of how well patients do fighting life-threatening diseases when they primarily rely on the FDA for safety verification and then make informed decisions, advised by their doctors, about accessing the most innovative new drugs on the Free To Choose track. This heretofore missing feedback would, I believe, compel the FDA to radically streamline its testing process with a concomitant reduction in regulatory costs for drug developers. In addition, the demonstrated benefits of early access would put public pressure on the FDA to learn how to better utilize observational data in order to grant observational approval, which would expedite insurance reimbursements. If the FDA doesn't want to take on the analytical challenge of working with TEDD's observational data, it could contract the analysis of TEDD data to the private sector.

If I have persuaded you that Free To Choose Medicine would make the world a better place, it may be because I've suggested a different worldview with which to perceive the FDA and the way forward to achieve better drugs, sooner, at lower cost. More and more people are concluding that the status-quo FDA monopoly is unacceptable. As of this writing, Colorado has passed, and other states will likely soon pass, Right To Try legislation that gives terminally ill patients the right to access drugs not approved by the FDA. Although this state legislation may not survive as a means to circumvent federal law, it has garnered substantial popular support because it represents common sense.

The goal of people living longer, healthier, and more productive lives is so powerful and universal that the rest of the world isn't waiting for leadership from the United States. Japan, with its aging population, has recently passed legislation that will allow patients to receive regenerative-medicine drugs that have passed safety trials but have not as yet clinically demonstrated efficacy. This is certainly in the spirit of Free To Choose Medicine.

It's likely that a bill to implement the key principles of Free To Choose Medicine will soon be introduced in Congress. After that occurs, you may want to contact your representatives in Congress and urge their support for this legislation.

Implementation of Free To Choose Medicine would be a defining moment for America—a change in direction from the current trend toward increasing regulation and litigation and a stake in the ground that control of medical decisions belongs, first and foremost, with individual patients and doctors, and not government.

## Key points
- Our current drugs-to-patients system, developed over the last fifty years, has been guided by the FDA's demands for more and more extensive clinical testing. Historically, changes to the system have been incremental and always implemented by the FDA itself. If we continue down this path, we will most assuredly not achieve order-of-magnitude improvement in the drugs-to-patients system.

- However, once information about the benefits of Free To Choose Medicine is more widely disseminated, perhaps the many groups fighting for incremental change within the current FDA environment will raise their sights and back Free To Choose Medicine.

- There are huge wealth-creation opportunities to be had from a new American industry focused on (1) facilitating data transmission from doctors involved with patient treatment results from using Free To Choose (not-yet-approved) drugs, (2) improving biopharmaceutical R&D from patient data (including genetic makeup and biomarkers) that would be part of a new observational database, and (3) analyzing and distributing information that significantly advances personalized medicine.

- To see how a world of Free To Choose Medicine would work, do an Internet search on "myTomorrows.com explained." This will lead you to an informative four-minute video produced by an innovative firm in the Netherlands that has recently successfully implemented a simplified version of Free To Choose Medicine on a small scale in parts of Europe.

# CHAPTER 7

# WORLDVIEWS AND EDUCATION

A traditional explanation for the persistent poverty of many less developed countries is that they lack objects such as natural resources or capital goods. But Taiwan started with little of either and still grew rapidly. Something else must be involved. Increasingly, emphasis is shifting to the notion that it is ideas, not objects, that poor countries lack. The knowledge needed to provide citizens of the poorest countries with a vastly improved standard of living already exists in the advanced countries. If a poor nation invests in education and does not destroy the incentives for its citizens to acquire ideas from the rest of the world, it can rapidly take advantage of the publicly available part of the worldwide stock of knowledge. If, in addition, it offers incentives for privately held ideas to be put to use within its borders—for example, by protecting foreign patents, copyrights, and licenses, by permitting direct investment by foreign firms, by protecting property rights, and by avoiding heavy regulation and high marginal tax rates—its citizens can soon work in state-of-the-art productive activities.

—Paul M. Romer
"Economic Growth"

## Summary of the core beliefs

Society benefits from business firms competing. Not only do consumers benefit from better products and services, but also resources continually move to their best use. In this competitive environment, the primary goal of firms is to efficiently provide value to customers. And since business firms compete, the goal then becomes providing higher value and/or achieving greater operational efficiency than one's competitors. This, in turn, involves a continual effort to be smarter than one's competitors. Getting smarter, as a practical matter, involves continually identifying faulty assumptions and generating new ideas that lead to improved problem-solving, more innovation, and enhanced value creation. Getting smarter is the purpose of reconstructing your worldview—and you can do this by incorporating the four, interrelated core beliefs.

**Core Belief 1: Past experiences shape assumptions.** Our perceptions are rooted in assumptions that are based on what has proved useful in the past and are typically based on an application of linear cause-and-effect analysis (if $X$, then $Y$). However, an automatic reliance on our assumptions can inadvertently lead to bad decisions, especially so whenever a significant change in context occurs.

**Core Belief 2: Language is perception's silent partner.** Our perceptions, our thinking, and our use of language are intertwined to such a degree that unraveling the assumptions "behind the words" can be a useful step in building knowledge. This also facilitates a creative use of language to generate new opportunities for a future unshackled from obsolete assumptions.

**Core Belief 3: Improve performance by identifying and fixing a system's key constraints.** Systems thinking is invaluable as a means to complement linear cause-and-effect analysis applied to isolated components of a system, to address the tendency toward an excessive focus on local efficiencies that can easily degrade over-all system performance, and to powerfully identify and focus on fixing the key constraints to achieving the system goal.

**Core Belief 4: Behavior is control of perception.** Human behavior is purposeful, so it can be productively analyzed as a living control system that acts to maintain the perceptions of important variables as close as possible to preferred levels. In short, behavior is control of perception. A control perspective reveals the underlying weakness in viewing the world primarily as stimulus-response experiences.

In my opinion, the more each of a society's members incorporates these core beliefs into his or her worldview, the greater the resulting dynamism, economic growth, and sustained job creation. This will lead to the development and delivery of new, innovative products and services; redesigned institutions; and innovative ways to motivate and organize people. Consequently, we would all benefit if our educational system were focused to a far greater degree on improving worldviews. Is there any evidence of such a change taking shape? Yes. In this chapter I'll describe ongoing initiatives that enable people to experience the benefits from improving their worldviews in ways that utilize one or more of the core beliefs.

## Business schools

This book began by focusing on how each of us participates in creating what we perceive as reality. Such a subtle, seemingly philosophical point has, as I've discussed, huge practical implications. Professor H. Thomas Johnson at Portland State University in Oregon explains the cultural shift in management and business schools as follows:

> At first the abstract information compiled and transmitted by these computer systems merely supplemented the perspectives of managers who were

already familiar with concrete details of the operations they managed, no matter how complicated and confused those operations became. Such individuals, prevalent in top management ranks before 1970, had a clear sense of the difference between "the map" created by abstract computer calculations and "the territory" that people inhabited in the workplace. Increasingly after 1970, however, managers lacking in shop floor experience or in engineering training, often trained in graduate business schools, came to dominate American and European manufacturing establishments. In their hands the "map was the territory." In other words, they considered reality to be the abstract quantitative models, the management accounting reports, and the computer scheduling algorithms.[1]

This observation reaffirms the hugely important but subtle influence of how managers perceive the world—what Erhard and Jensen refer to as the "occurring world." Language, which of course is employed in such diverse ways as quantitative models, accounting reports, and so on, plays a decidedly important role in how we view the world around us. It makes sense that as our business language becomes more sophisticated, the more confident we tend to become both in our initial assessment of problem situations and in our proposed solutions. In the case of business-school students, as they become more skillful in both the language and the logic of their classroom work, they become more successful in giving correct answers on tests. Yet the preeminent problem-solvers featured in this book uniformly lacked confidence in automatically accepting assumptions, especially those assumptions formulated with little regard for changing context. These notable thinkers were determined to gain insights from experimental data—feedback—and had a passion for learning from mistakes.

Business students are immersed in a classroom environment in which lecturers demonstrate their mastery of the mathematics of elegant and parsimonious theories as well as the logic of myriad principles in finance, accounting, and other core subjects. The better students become when applying such abstract knowledge on tests, the better their grades. In contrast, Ray Dalio, featured in Chapter 3, points out that often graduates from the top schools are good "school learners" but bad "mistake learners" in real-world situations, since their education was all about getting the right answers on tests. Jim Womack, discussed in Chapter 4, reminisces about his transition from being in his office applying theory to easily available data to immersing himself in the *gemba*, where the actual work takes place, in order to generate useful hypotheses about ways to improve performance by drilling down to understand the root causes of problems.

The use of language can help or hinder how we understand cause and effect in complex situations. For example, when faced with analyzing the crash of Alaska Airlines flight 261, as covered in Chapter 3, most people would be highly likely to talk about the "problem" as determining whether "pilot error" or "mechanical failure" was *the* cause. The words in quotes in the previous sentence signify major barriers to learning—barriers that are seldom questioned or even perceived. Absent Core Belief 2, which instills the habit of skepticism about language, a typical researcher simply mushes ahead, unconcerned about the assumptions hidden behind the words. And would not the "facts" about the failure of the jackscrew unit seal the deal as to what "caused" the crash? Yet the real cause, as previously discussed, was in how the world occurred to Alaska Airlines management and maintenance personnel over many years. Language matters and it especially matters in complex business situations.

## Innovative educational initiatives

The summary that follows highlights some educational initiatives, which are plowing new ground and which serve as current examples of the application of improved worldviews, reflecting the spirit of this book.[2]

In 2008 Chapman University in California made a bet that has paid huge dividends in improving the education of its students. That year, the Economic Science Institute (ESI) was established at Chapman as a research center for Vernon Smith and his team of experimental economists. ESI researchers use the laboratory method of inquiry to investigate the role that human institutions play in creating wealth, and also to build and test market-based management systems (as discussed in Chapter 2). ESI's research spans the fields of accounting, economics, finance, information systems, engineering, psychology, neuroscience, computer science, and philosophy. Additionally, Chapman's Argyros School of Business and Economics incorporates the experimental mindset into its courses for business students. Chapman offers a master of science degree in economic systems design, which offers unique benefits as compared with a more traditional theory-based degree. The University of Chicago, the University of Virginia, and other schools now provide classes in which students actively participate in learning about experimental economics.

DePaul University in Chicago recently introduced the four core beliefs in its strategy courses and in a new MBA capstone course, "Integrated Strategic Analysis for Competing Globally." The courses are offered as part of the Center for Strategy, Execution and Valuation in the Kellstadt Graduate School of Business, which uses an innovative approach in business schools by integrating the fields of strategy, strategy execution, and valuation. This approach was designed to avoid the disadvantages inherent in the silo-based focus prevalent in most business school curriculums. The introduction of the four core beliefs and reconstructed worldview described in this book were a valuable addition to this integrated curriculum.

Werner Erhard, Michael Jensen, and their Barbados Group colleagues (EJB) are developing a new paradigm for improving performance (as highlighted in Chapter 3) and creating an innovative leadership course. Their approach stresses how constraints imposed by one's own worldview can impede cognitive abilities that would otherwise be available. Instead of just learning about leadership, their goal is for course participants to overcome constraints and achieve ontological mastery—by *being* leaders.

As previously discussed, EJB's work emphasizes that your actions are naturally correlated with the ways in which situations occur to you. Leadership is often about the realization of a distinctly better future than the current situation, in which expectations can be firmly rooted in past experiences. (This orientation is similar to Eli Goldratt's TOC "current reality tree" and "future reality tree.") Leveraging EJB's work via adoption in mainstream business school curriculums will take some effort, but the potential payoff is considerable.[3]

Stanford University's d.school was briefly highlighted in Chapter 3 in the example of the four students who developed a baby warmer that cost 99 percent less than a conventional incubator. Founded by David Kelley of IDEO, the d.school teaches students from a broad range of disciplines about how to use design thinking to collaboratively deliver innovative solutions for complex and difficult problems in any field. Design thinking is consistent in general with the knowledge-building loop (as illustrated in Figure 3.1) although the terminology differs: "empathize and define" versus my "purposes and worldview"; "ideate and prototype" versus "perceptions, actions, and consequences"; and "test" versus "feedback."

Much of the intellectual content of this book ties into what students experience in the hands-on, action-oriented environment of the d.school. For example, design thinking stresses in the extreme the need to empathize with the users of a product or service, and that involves extraordinarily detailed, even anthropological observations of people and their environment. Sound familiar to Ohno's circle?

It is encouraging that the d.school's successes have motivated the leaders of other universities to offer classes that focus on design thinking. Especially notable is the curriculum-wide integration of design thinking by the Rotman School of Management at the University of Toronto.[4] The former dean of the Rotman School, Roger Martin, who orchestrated the transformation of this business school, explained the importance of design thinking as follows:

> We are on the cusp of a design revolution in business. Competing is no longer about creating dominance in scale-intensive industries, it's about producing elegant, refined products and services in imagination-intensive industries. *As a result, business people don't just need to understand designers better—they need to become designers.*[5]

## Concluding thoughts

I hope that your reading of the earlier chapters led you to conclude that Core Beliefs 1, 2, and 3 are straightforward and logical. But Core Belief 4—behavior is control of perception—may strike you as more complex. In my own case, reaching a comfort level entailed a considerable amount of research in order to "get it." Consequently, my goal for Chapter 5 was to substantially shorten the time needed for others to "get" the intellectual power of Perceptual Control Theory.

I have been on a long intellectual journey studying worldviews as practiced by those who solve especially challenging problems and getting my thinking straight on a wide variety of complex issues related to how we know what we think we know. I hope this book will provide ideas that quicken the pace for those wanting to improve their worldviews in order to better handle complex problems. My sense is that a restructured worldview that actively applies the four core beliefs will translate into significant performance improvements in both one's work life and one's personal life. On a larger scale, as one attains more of a leadership role in a group, organization, or business enterprise, one can leverage an improved worldview through wealth-creating actions that make for a better future for oneself as well as for others.

Along the lines of a better future, what are the ingredients for finding a truly big-impact project that can lead to an order-of-magnitude improvement in performance? My answer: find a situation where the "way we do things around here" is rarely, if ever, seriously questioned; where that way of doing things involves one or more assumptions that sound plausible, even bulletproof, but were formulated a long time ago for a different environment than that which exists today; and where the status-quo has a veneer of efficiency that disappears when a total systems approach is applied and/or when a deeper understanding of customers reveals a significant opportunity to increase value delivered to them. As you've probably gathered, it seems to me that the Free To Choose Medicine project, which I discuss in Chapter 6, is a solution for just such a situation.

If *Reconstructing Your Worldview* meets with success, it will be because I've managed to provide my readers with a fast and efficient way to improve their ability to analyze complex, important problems and to make better decisions. The best way to implement the ideas in this book is not just to think in an abstract manner about the material. Rather, be extraordinarily attentive to the assumptions behind the words, observe problem situations firsthand in minute detail, ask "why?" repeatedly in a systematic drilling-down to discover root causes of problems, and regularly experiment. In this manner, you will both experience and demonstrate the practical value of an improved worldview to yourself and to others.

I wish you success.

# NOTES

## Introduction

1. Details of my correspondence with Friedman regarding his research methodology are posted at http://learningwhatworks. com/papers/MiltonFriedman%20_2_.pdf. See also my article Madden (1991).

## Chapter 1

1. Gazzaniga, Ivry, and Mangun (2008).
2. Eagleman (2011).
3. Jeff Hawkins's (2004) memory-prediction theory asserts that the neocortex, which occupies 75 percent of the volume of the brain, uses the same mechanism to process all sensory information and is central to any theory of how our brains function. Hawkins's theory is consistent with accepted scientific knowledge that the neocortex is composed of a similar structure throughout its layers. He argues that the neocortex is actually a memory system, which processes information in a hierarchical fashion, and which ties into the material presented in Chapter 5 on Perceptual Control Theory. Instead of "solving" problems, it retrieves answers from memory. The neocortex sends information both up and down its hierarchical organization so that feedback can compare prediction to actual results. In Hawkins's words (2004, p. 113):

> For many years most scientists ignored these
> feedback connections. If your understanding of
> the brain focused on how the cortex took input,

processed it, and then acted on it, you didn't need feedback. All you needed were feedforward connections leading from sensory to motor sections of the cortex. But when you begin to realize that the cortex's core function is to make predictions, then you have to put feedback into the model; the brain has to send information flowing back toward the region that first receives the inputs. Prediction requires a comparison between what is happening and what you expect to happen. What is actually happening flows up, and what you expect to happen flows down.

Of particular interest is Hawkins's mission to develop computer programs that "think and learn" consistent with the hierarchical theory of how the brain works. Such programs may yield an order of magnitude improvement in dealing with problems that involve the interpretation of a huge amount of real-time data (see www.numenta.org).

4. Gregory (2009, p. 10).

5. Frith (2007, pp. 17, 132).

6. The concept of individuals participating in creating their own "reality," as opposed to an independent reality, was central to John Dewey's later work in philosophy. Dewey had a strong influence on Adelbert Ames, Jr., who pioneered innovative visual demonstrations that clearly showed the effect of one's assumptions, based on past experiences, on perceptions of the world out there (Bamberger [2006], Kilpatrick [1961], and Madden [2011]). For an insightful window into the thinking of Ames, including correspondence with Dewey, see Cantril (1960). In contrast to the endless arguments in the academic literature about perception and the role of assumptions, a personal exposure to some of the Ames Demonstrations is a unique, insightful experience. The Explor-

atorium in San Francisco is open to the public and has a working demonstration of the Ames Distorted Room, which even today is still discussed in psychology textbooks.

## Chapter 2

1. Attributed to R. D. Laing. See Crain, Seymour, and Crockett, 1993, p. 53.
2. Figure 2.1 is an Evaporating Cloud application of the Theory of Constraints (Cox and Schleier, 2010) thinking tools discussed in Chapter 4.
3. Worldviews evolve through experience. For a discussion of Walmart's growth, see Walton (1992) and Chapter 4 of Hurst (2012). Hurst notes (p. 37):

> Walton had to develop his own, highly efficient distribution system because traditional wholesalers refused to make small drop-offs on remote country routes. This was the genesis of the company's famed logistics system, which gradually evolved as the constraints to efficient shipping were steadily overcome by novel solutions, such as cross-docking, where goods coming in from suppliers are shipped directly to branches, and then further refined.

    In his book, Hurst argues that the mind is rational in an ecological sense, i.e., it has evolved to extract cues to action from specific situations. Context matters, and for managers "the ability to design, evoke, control, anticipate, and counter contexts may be the most powerful skill that you have" (p. 9).
4. Rumelt (2011).
5. Vance and Scott (1994).
6. Turner (2003); Basker (2007).
7. Dupas (2011).
8. Johnson (2006).
9. Phelps (2013), p. vii.

10. Phelps (2013), pp. x and xi.
11. Mokyr (2014).
12. Smith (2008); Plott and Smith (2008).
13. Rassenti, Smith, and Wilson (2002).
14. Smith (1989).
15. Debre (1998); Tiner (1990).
16. Bertrand and Mullainathan (2004).
17. Gneezy, List, and Price (2012).
18. Gneezy and List (2013), p. 244.

## Chapter 3

1. This quotation is from the Foreword to Brothers (2005).
2. Madden (1991).
3. The importance of context was succinctly summarized in Barsalou, Wilson, and Hasenkamp (2010), pp. 334 and 344, as follows:

> When a phenomenon is studied carefully, it typically does not behave the same way across contexts. Regardless of whether the phenomenon is genetic, neural, cognitive, behavioral, social, or cultural, it is likely to exhibit extensive sensitivity to context ... nouns are often associated with process simplification [eliminate context] ... both lay public and scientists exhibit strong predispositions to view the world through the lens of simple, objectified noun concepts. Contrary to this view, extensive evidence exists that the world does not work this way. Instead, the fundamental building blocks of everything, from genetics to culture, appear to be dynamic, context-sensitive processes.

4. Dekker (2005), pp. 2, 4, and 5.
5. Starbuck and Milliken (1988).
6. Dekker (2006).

7. Rodriguez (2006).
8. Bazin (2000), p. 39.
9. http://www.fastcompany.com/52795/strategy-design.
10. http://www.bwater.com/home/culture-principles.aspx.
11. Schwager (2012).
12. Barbados Group's working papers are posted at http://ssrn.com/link/barbados-group.html.
13. In *Sleights of Mind: What the Neuroscience of Magic Reveals About Our Everyday Deceptions*, Stephen L. Macknik and Susana Martinez-Conde note (pp. 8–13) the following:

> Your expectations are based on all of your prior experiences and memories. What you see in the here and now is what proved useful to you in the past ... magicians understand at a deeply intuitive level that you alone create your experience of reality ... they exploit the fact that your brain does a staggering amount of outright confabulation in order to construct the mental simulation of reality known as "consciousness" ... you believe you are aware of your surroundings, but at any given moment you're blocking out 95 percent of all that is happening ... the richness of your visual experience is an illusion created by the filling-in processes of your brain.

14. Erhard, Jensen, and the Barbados Group (2010), pp. 49 and 52.
15. Winograd and Flores (1986).
16. Jensen (2009).
17. Smith (2000), p. 4.

## Chapter 4
1. Sterman (2000).
2. Graham, Harvey, and Rajgopal (2006); Jensen (2003).
3. Womack and Jones (2003), p. 20.

4. Ohno (1988), p. ix.
5. May (2006), p. 73.
6. Womack (2011), p. 70.
7. Madden (1993).
8. Dettmer (2007); Cox and Schleier (2010); Goldratt and Goldratt-Ashlag (2010); Scheinkopf (2010).
9. The management of Pipeline Trading Systems developed its approach for *institutional* investors independently of my published article. The only significant difference was that I envisioned both *retail and institutional* investors interacting. Also, it is not at all clear whether trading exchanges want to provide the technology that would enable retail investors who trade in significant size to interact with institutional investors. The alternative, especially for retail investors with sizable orders, is the time-consuming management of a continual stream of small-limit orders that are profitable for exchanges even if the result is an inefficient process for retail investors. Moreover, today's high-frequency traders receive favorable treatment by the exchanges to the disadvantage of investors using limit orders.
10. Clark (1998), p. 51.
11. Resnick (1997), p. 120.
12. Hayek (1945).

## Chapter 5

1. In an 1896 article in *Psychological Review,* John Dewey explained the circular loop of stimulus-response as follows: "What we have is a circuit, not an arc or broken segment of a circle. This circuit is more truly termed organic than reflex, because the motor response determines the stimulus, just as truly as sensory stimulus determines movement." Dewey (1896).
2. Powers (2005), p. 312.

3. In their 2013 book, *Computational and Robotic Models of the Hierarchical Organization of Behavior,* Gianluca Baldassarre and Marco Mirolli summarize:

> The hierarchical organization of behavior is a fundamental means through which robots and organisms can acquire and produce sophisticated and flexible behaviors that allow them to solve multiple tasks in multiple conditions. Recently, the research on this topic has been receiving increasing attention. On the one hand, machine learning and robotics are recognizing the fundamental importance of the hierarchical organization of behavior for building robots that scale up to solve complex tasks.... On the other hand, research in psychology and neuroscience is finding increasing evidence that modularity and hierarchy are pivotal organization principles of behavior and of the brain.

4. After digesting the material in Chapter 5, you are likely to see PCT connections to the research findings reported in *The Progress Principle: Using Small Wins to Ignite Joy, Engagement, and Creativity at Work* by Teresa Amabile and Steven Kramer. The authors note the following:

> Conventional management wisdom is way off track about employee psychology. When we surveyed hundreds of managers around the world, ranging from CEOs to project leaders, about what motivates employees, we found startling results: 95 percent of these leaders fundamentally misunderstood the most important source of motivation. Our research inside companies revealed that the best way to motivate people, day in and day out, is by facilitating *progress*—even small wins. But the managers in our survey

ranked "supporting progress" dead last as a work motivator. [p. 3]

… When you do what it takes to facilitate progress in work people care about, managing them—and managing the organization—becomes much more straightforward. You don't need to parse people's psyches or tinker with their incentives, because helping them succeed at making a difference virtually guarantees good inner work life *and* strong performance. It's more cost-effective than relying on massive incentives, too. When you don't manage for progress, no amount of emotional intelligence or incentive planning will save the day. [p. 10]

5. Bernard (1957).
6. James (1952), p. 4.
7. Mayr (1970).
8. In their article "A century of psychology and psychotherapy: Is an understanding of 'control' the missing link between theory, research, and practice?" Warren Mansell and Timothy Carey point out:

The ability to view the brain in action forces us to confront some basic truths—we are biological beings—and what we call "beliefs," "attitudes" or even "working memory" do not exist in the same tangible sense as a chair or a duck; they are essentially functions carried out by coordinated networks of cells that form the brain. William James took a functionalist view of the mind, which seems apparent in today's cutting edge science. Interestingly, it is now established that throughout the sensory cortex, the neural pathways sending signals down from higher order areas of the brain, such as the frontal regions, are at least as substantial as those sending signal in the traditional, "input" direction. It seems that at every level of perception, top-down information is utilized, or integrated in some way, with incoming signals from the sensory organs. While this evidence fits with cognitive approaches, it is particularly consistent with a view of the brain as a purposeful organ that guides and regulates incoming perception.

9. There is a great deal of published material on PCT. Listed below are suggested readings, beginning with the most basic and leading to more advanced technical material.

   a) A useful beginning point is to visit these websites: http://www.pctweb.org, http://www.iapct.org, and www.livingcontrolsystems.com.

   b) Bill Powers (1998) is an easy-to-read PCT overview. Powers (2005) is the classic statement about PCT. Cziko (2000) describes how PCT connects to the work of Claude Bernard and Charles Darwin. Yin (2013) provides an insightful discussion of the role of PCT in restoring purpose in behavior.

   c) Marken (1992, 2002); Runkel (2003); Forssell (2009).

   d) Powers (1989, 1992, 2008).

10. For an application of PCT to sociology see McClelland and Fararo (2006). See Carey (2006) for a method of psychotherapy based on PCT principles.

## Chapter 6

1. A refinement to the Free To Choose Medicine proposal described in Madden (2012) is detailed in Conko and Madden (2013). Specifically, a drug manufacturer could request to put a not-yet-approved drug on the Free To Choose track after one or more Phase II trials are successfully completed.

This would provide an early-access path to begin before completion of all Phase II trials for new drugs that generate exceptional efficacy early in Phase II trials. Chapter 6 is consistent with this refinement.

2. Three committees (Levelt, Noorth, and Drenth) issued a report, "Flawed Science: The fraudulent research practices of social psychologist Diederik Stapel," available at http://editorethics.uncc.edu/PDF/_finalreportlevet-1.pdf.

3. Trowbridge and Walker (2007).

4. Huber (2013), pp. 101–102.

5. http://www.abigail-alliance.org, accessed February 24, 2014.

6. Boger (2012).

7. Von Eschenbach (2012).

## Chapter 7

1. Johnson and Bröms (2000), p. 25.

2. That business schools are in need of innovation is documented by Khurana (2007); Locke and Spender (2011); and Datar, Garvin, and Cullen (2010).

3. Erhard, Jensen, and Granger (2011).

4. For an overview of the educational approach offered by the Rotman School of Management see Datar, Garvin, and Cullen (2010), pp. 131–136.

5. Martin and Christensen (2013), p. 9.

# REFERENCES

Amabile, Teresa, and Steven Kramer. 2011. *The Progress Principle: Using Small Wins to Ignite Joy, Engagement, and Creativity at Work.* Boston: Harvard Business Review Press.

Baldassarre, Gianluca, and Marco Mirolli, eds. 2013. *Computational and Robotic Models of the Hierarchical Organization of Behavior.* New York: Springer.

Bamberger, W. C. 2006. *Adelbert Ames, Jr.: A Life of Vision and Becomingness.* Whitmore Lake, MI: Bamberger Books.

Barsalou, Laurence W., Christine D. Wilson, and Wendy Hasenkamp. 2010. "On the Vices of Nominalization and the Virtues of Contextualizing." In Batja Mesquita, Lisa Feldman Barrett, and Eliot R. Smith, eds., *The Mind In Context.* New York: Guilford Press.

Basker, E. 2007. "The causes and consequences of Walmart's growth." *Journal of Economic Perspectives* 21(3): 177–198.

Bazin, Hervé. 2000. *The Eradication of Smallpox.* London: Academic Press.

Bernard, Claude. 1957. *An Introduction to the Study of Experimental Medicine.* Mineola, NY: Dover Publications.

Bertrand, Marianne, and Sendhil Mullainathan. 2004. "Are Emily and Greg More Employable Than Lakisha and Jamal? A Field Experiment on Labor Market Discrimination." *American Economic Review* 94(4): 991–1013.

Boger, Joshua. 2012. "To boost R&D, stop flying blind and start observing." *Beyond Borders: Global Biotechnology Report*, pp. 22–23. Ernst & Young.

Brothers, Chalmers. 2005. *Language and the Pursuit of Happiness.* Naples, FL: New Possibilities Press.

Cantril, Hadley, ed. 1960. *The Morning Notes of Adelbert Ames, Jr.* New Brunswick, NJ: Rutgers University Press.

Carey, Timothy A. 2006. *The Method of Levels.* Hayward, CA: Living Control Systems Publishing.

Clark, Andy. 1998. *Being There: Putting Brain, Body, and World Together Again.* Cambridge, MA: MIT Press.

Conko, Gregory, and Bartley J. Madden. 2013. "Free To Choose Medicine." *Engage.* 14(3): 4–13.

Cox, James F., and John G. Schleier, Jr., eds. 2010. *Theory of Constraints Handbook.* New York: McGraw-Hill.

Crain, Margaret Ann, Jack L. Seymour, and Joseph Crockett. 1993. *Educating Christians: The Intersection of Meaning, Learning, and Vocation.* Nashville, TN: Abingdon Press.

Cziko, Gary. 2000. *The Things We Do: Using the Lessons of Bernard and Darwin to Understand the What, How, and Why of Our Behavior.* Cambridge, MA: MIT Press.

Datar, Srikant M., David A. Garvin, and Patrick G. Cullen. 2010. *Rethinking the MBA.* Boston: Harvard Business Press.

Debre, Patrice. 1998. *Louis Pasteur.* Baltimore: Johns Hopkins University Press.

Dekker, Sidney. 2005. *Ten Questions About Human Error.* Mahwah, NJ: Lawrence Erlbaum Associates, Publishers.

Dekker, Sidney. 2006. *The Field Guide to Understanding Human Error.* Burlington, VT: Ashgate Publishing Company.

Dettmer, H. William. 2007. *The Logical Thinking Process: A Systems Approach to Complex Problem Solving.* Milwaukee, WI: ASQ Quality Press.

Dewey, John. 1896. "The reflex arc concept in psychology." *Psychological Review* 3: 357–370.

Dupas, Pascaline. 2011. "Do Teenagers Respond to HIV Risk Information? Evidence from a Field Experiment in Kenya." *American Economic Journal: Applied Economics* 3 (January): 1–34.

Eagleman, David. 2011. *Incognito: The Secret Lives of the Brain.* New York: Pantheon Books.

Erhard, Werner, Michael C. Jensen, and the Barbados Group. 2010. "A New Paradigm of Individual, Group, and Organizational Performance." Working paper available at http://ssrn.com/abstract=1437027.

Erhard, Werner, Michael C. Jensen, and Kari L. Granger. 2011. "Creating Leaders: An Ontological Model." Forthcoming in Scott Snook, Nitin Nohria, Rakesh Khurana, eds. *The Handbook for Teaching Leadership.* Sage Publications. Available at http://ssrn.com/abstract=1681682.

Forrester, Jay W. 1969. *Urban Dynamics.* Cambridge, MA: MIT Press.

Forssell, Dag, ed. 2009. *Perceptual Control Theory: Science & Applications, A Book of Readings.* Hayward, CA: Living Control Systems Publishing.

Frith, Chris. 2007. *Making Up the Mind: How the Brain Creates Our Mental World.* Hoboken, NJ: John Wiley & Sons.

Gazzaniga, Michael S., Richard B. Ivry, and George R. Mangun. 2008. *Cognitive Neuroscience: The Biology of the Mind*, 3rd ed. New York: W. W. Norton.

Gneezy, Uri, John A. List, and Michael K. Price. 2012. "Toward an Understanding of Why People Discriminate: Evidence from a Series of Natural Field Experiments." NBER Working Paper 17855.

Gneezy, Uri, and John A. List. 2013. *The Why Axis: Hidden Motives and the Undiscovered Economics of Everyday Life*. New York: PublicAffairs.

Goldratt, Eliyahu M., and Jeff Cox. 2004. *The Goal: A Process of Ongoing Improvement*, 3rd ed. Great Barrington, MA: North River Press.

Goldratt, Eliyahu M., and Efrat Goldratt-Ashlag. 2010. *The Choice*. Great Barrington, MA: North River Press.

Graham, John R., Campbell R. Harvey, and Shivaram Rajgopal. 2006. "Value Destruction and Financial Reporting Decisions." *Financial Analysts Journal* 62, 6 (November/December): 27–39.

Gregory, Richard L. 2009. *Seeing Through Illusions*. Oxford: Oxford University Press.

Hawkins, Jeff. 2004. *On Intelligence*. New York: Times Books.

Hayek, Friedrich A. 1945. "The Use of Knowledge in Society." *American Economic Review* 35(4): 519–530.

Huber, Peter W. 2013. *The Cure in the Code: How 20th Century Law Is Undermining 21st Century Medicine*. New York: Basic Books.

Hurst, David K. 2012. *The New Ecology of Leadership: Business Mastery in a Chaotic World*. New York: Columbia University Press.

James, William. 1952. *The Principles of Psychology*. Chicago: Encyclopaedia Britannica.

Jensen, Michael C. 2003. "Paying People to Lie: The Truth About the Budgeting Process." *European Financial Management* 9(3): 379–406. Available at http://ssrn.com/abstract=267651.

Jensen, Michael C. 2009. "Integrity: Without It Nothing Works." *Rotman: The Magazine of the Rotman School of Management*. Fall: 16–20.

Johnson, Steven. 2006. *The Ghost Map: The Story of London's Most Terrifying Epidemic—and How It Changed Science, Cities, and the Modern World*. New York: Riverhead Books.

Johnson, Thomas H., and Andre Bröms. 2000. *Profit Beyond Measure: Extraordinary Results Through Attention to Process and People*. New York: Free Press.

Khurana, Rakesh. 2007. *From Higher Aims to Hired Hands: The Social Transformation of American Business Schools and the Unfilled Promise of Management as a Profession*. Princeton: Princeton University Press.

Kilpatrick, Franklin P., ed. 1961. *Explorations in Transactional Psychology*. New York: New York University Press.

Locke, Robert R., and J. C. Spender. 2011. *Confronting Managerialism: How the Business Elite and Their Schools Threw Our Lives Out of Balance*. London: Zed Books.

Macknik, Stephen L., and Susana Martinez-Conde. 2010. *Sleights of Mind: What the Neuroscience of Magic Reveals About Our Everyday Deceptions*. New York: Henry Holt and Company.

Madden, Bartley J. 1991. "A Transactional Approach to Economic Research." *Journal of Socio-Economics* 20(1): 57–71. Available at http://learningwhatworks.com/papers/transactional%20 approach.pdf.

Madden, Bartley J. 1993. "Structural Changes in Trading Stocks." *Journal of Portfolio Management* 20(1): 19–27.

Madden, Bartley J. 2010. *Wealth Creation: A Systems Mindset for Building and Investing in Businesses for the Long Term.* Hoboken, NJ: John Wiley & Sons.

Madden, Bartley J. 2011. "Management's Knowing Process and the Theory of Constraints." Working paper available at http://ssrn.com/abstract=1806500.

Madden, Bartley J. 2012. *Free To Choose Medicine: Better Drugs Sooner at Lower Cost,* 2nd ed. Naperville, IL: LearningWhatWorks.

Mansell, Warren, and Timothy A. Carey. 2009. "A century of psychology and psychotherapy: Is an understanding of 'control' the missing link between theory, research, and practice?" *Psychology and Psychotherapy: Theory, Research, and Practice* 82: 337–353.

Marken, Richard S. 1992. *Mind Readings: Experimental Studies of Purpose.* Durango, CO: Control Systems Group.

Marken, Richard S. 2002. *More Mind Readings: Methods and Models in the Study of Purpose.* St. Louis, MO: newview.

Marken, Richard S. 2009. "You Say You Had a Revolution: Methodological Foundations of Closed Loop Psychology." *Review of General Psychology* 13(2): 137–145.

Martin, Roger, and Karen Christensen. 2013. *Rotman on Design.* Toronto: University of Toronto Press.

May, Matthew E. 2006. *The Elegant Solution: Toyota's Formula for Mastering Innovation.* New York: Free Press.

Mayr, Otto. 1970. *The Origins of Feedback Control.* Cambridge, MA: MIT Press.

McClelland, Kent A., and Thomas J. Fararo, eds. 2006. *Purpose, Meaning, and Action.* New York: Palgrave Macmillan.

Mokyr, Joel. 2014. "A Flourishing Economist: A Review Essay on Edmund Phelps' *Mass Flourishing: How Grassroots Innovation Created Jobs, Challenges, and Change.*" *Journal of Economic Literature* 52(1): 189–196.

North, Douglas C. 2005. *Understanding the Process of Economic Change.* Princeton, NJ: Princeton University Press.

Ohno, Taiichi. 1988. *Toyota Production System: Beyond Large-Scale Production.* New York: Productivity Press.

Phelps, Edmund. 2013. *Mass Flourishing: How Grassroots Innovation Created Jobs, Challenge, and Change.* Princeton, NJ: Princeton University Press.

Plott, Charles R., and Vernon L. Smith. 2008. *Handbook of Experimental Economics Results.* Amsterdam: North-Holland.

Powers, William T. 1989. *Living Control Systems.* Gravel Switch, KY: Control Systems Group.

Powers, William T. 1992. *Living Control Systems II.* Gravel Switch, KY: Control Systems Group.

Powers, William T. 1998. *Making Sense of Behavior.* New Canaan, CT: Benchmark Publications.

Powers, William T. 2001. "The Neglected Phenomenon of Negative Feedback Control." http://www.LivingControlSystems.com/intro_papers/neglected_phenomenon.pdf.

Powers, William T. 2005. *Behavior: The Control of Perception.* New Canaan, CT: Benchmark Publications.

Powers, William T. 2008. *Living Control Systems III: The Fact of Control.* Bloomfield, NJ: Benchmark Publications.

Rassenti, Stephen R., Vernon L. Smith, and Bart J. Wilson. 2002. "Using Experiments to Inform the Privatization/Deregulation Movement in Electricity." *Cato Journal* (Winter): 515–544.

Resnick, Mitchell. 1997. *Turtles, Termites, and Traffic Jams: Explorations in Massively Parallel Microworlds.* Cambridge, MA: MIT Press.

Rodriguez, Ana Maria. 2006. *Edward Jenner: Conqueror of Smallpox.* Berkeley Heights, NJ: Enslow Publishers.

Romer, Paul. 2008. "Economic Growth." In David R. Henderson, ed., *The Concise Encyclopedia of Economics.* Indianapolis, IN: Liberty Fund.

Rumelt, Richard P. 2011. *Good Strategy Bad Strategy: The Difference and Why It Matters.* New York: Crown Business.

Runkel, Philip J. 2003. *People as Living Things: The Psychology of Perceptual Control.* Hayward, CA: Living Control Systems Publishing.

Scheinkopf, Lisa J. 2010. "Thinking Processes Including S&T Trees." In James F. Cox and John G. Schleier, Jr., eds., *Theory of Constraints Handbook.* New York: McGraw-Hill Irwin.

Schwager, Jack. 2012. *Hedge Fund Market Wizards: How Winning Traders Win.* Hoboken, NJ: John Wiley & Sons.

Smith, Debra. 2000. *The Measurement Nightmare: How the Theory of Constraints Can Resolve Conflicting Strategies, Policies, and Measures.* New York: St. Lucie Press.

Smith, Vernon L. 1989. "Theory, Experiment and Economics." *Journal of Economic Perspectives* 3(1): 151–169.

Smith, Vernon L. 2008. *Rationality in Economics: Constructivist and Ecological Forms*. Cambridge: Cambridge University Press.

Starbuck, William H., and Frances J. Milliken. 1988. "Challenger: Fine Tuning the Odds Until Something Breaks." *Journal of Management Studies* 25: 319–340.

Sterman, John D. 2000. *Business Dynamics: Systems Thinking and Modeling for a Complex World*. New York: McGraw-Hill Irwin.

Tiner, John Hudson. 1990. *Louis Pasteur*. Milford, MI: Mott Media.

Trowbridge, Ronald L., and Steven Walker. "The FDA's Deadly Track Record." *Wall Street Journal*, August 14, 2007, p. A17.

Turner, Marcia Layton. 2003. *Kmart's Ten Deadly Sins: How Incompetence Tainted an American Icon*. Hoboken, NJ: John Wiley & Sons.

Vance, Sandra S., and Roy V. Scott. 1994. *Wal-Mart: A History of Sam Walton's Retail Phenomenon*. New York: Twayne Publishers.

Von Eschenbach, Andrew. "Medical Innovation: How the U.S. Can Retain Its Lead." *Wall Street Journal*, February 14, 2012.

Walton, Sam. 1992. *Sam Walton: Made in America: My Story*. New York: Doubleday.

Winograd, Terry, and Fernando Flores. 1986. *Understanding Computers and Cognition: A New Foundation for Design*. Reading, MA: Addison-Wesley.

Womack, James P., and Daniel T. Jones. 2003. *Lean Thinking: Banish Waste and Create Wealth in Your Corporation*, 2nd ed. New York: Free Press.

Womack, Jim. 2011. *Gemba Walks*. Cambridge, MA: Lean Enterprise Institute.

Yin, Henry H. "Restoring Purpose in Behavior." In Baldassarre and Mirolli (2013).

Zaffron, Steve, and Dave Logan. 2009. *The Three Laws of Performance: Rewriting the Future of Your Organization and Your Life*. San Francisco: Jossey-Bass.

# ACKNOWLEDGEMENTS

**IN THE EARLY** 1980s, I began a concerted effort to get a better handle on how we know what we think we know. The takeoff point was the work on a transactional approach to knowing by John Dewey and Arthur Bentley that explicitly recognized our participation in shaping the world that we see as real. This led me to studying the ingenious visual demonstrations of Adelbert Ames, Jr., and that became the foundation for Core Belief 1. For many years I benefited from exchanging ideas about technical issues in knowledge-building with Ernest Welker, an expert in the Dewey/Bentley approach and former director of research at the American Institute for Economic Research.

Another longtime collaborator is Marie Murray, a former journalism professor, who edited most of my published articles and books over the last twenty-five years. Marie spent considerable time on the logical underpinnings and language used in crafting this book. The final product substantially benefited from her insights.

Ideas to improve this book provided by Bob Hendricks, David Hurst, Tom Gruenwald, and Dag Forssell were especially beneficial. I also benefited from the comments provided by Susan Dudley, Jeff Madden, Alex Tabarrok, and Rawley Thomas.

The final manuscript was superbly edited by Lisa Pliscou and the production skillfully orchestrated by Holly Brady.

# ABOUT THE AUTHOR

**BARTLEY J. MADDEN** retired as a managing director of Credit Suisse/HOLT after a career in money management and investment research that included the founding of Callard Madden & Associates. His early research led to the development of the CFROI valuation framework that is used today by money-management firms worldwide.

Madden's current research focuses on knowledge-building and wealth creation as opposite sides of the same coin, and also on the application of the ideas in this book to public policy. For more on these topics, visit his website www.LearningWhatWorks.com. Additionally, the YouTube video "Reconstructing Your Worldview" provides insights about the four core beliefs central to this book and their application to solving complex problems. His view on the role of capitalism in making the world a better place is the subject of a forthcoming book and presented in the YouTube video "Capitalism and Management's Core Responsibilities." Madden's work in finance and systems thinking is summarized in his book *Wealth Creation: A Systems Mindset for Building and Investing in Businesses for the Long Term*.

Madden's proposal to restructure the Food and Drug Administration is presented in his book *Free To Choose Medicine: Better Drugs Sooner at Lower Cost*, which was developed in journal articles in *Regulation, Cancer Biotherapy & Radiopharmaceuticals*, and *Medical Hypotheses*. At the present time, the core Free To Choose Medicine principles of consumer choice and competition for the FDA are being implemented by various state governments via Right To Try legislation that is designed to enable patients, fighting life-threatening illnesses, to access not-yet-approved drugs.

Made in the USA
Middletown, DE
15 May 2015